The
Courage to
Speak Your Truth

The
Courage to
Speak Your Truth

Shifting The Narrative on Childhood Sexual Abuse

KATH ESSING

First published in 2025 by Dean Publishing
PO Box 119
Mt. Macedon, Victoria, 3441
Australia
deanpublishing.com

DEAN PUBLISHING

Cataloguing-in-Publication Data
National Library of Australia

Title: The Courage to Speak Your Truth
ISBN: 978-0-648-75806-8
Category: Family & Relationships / Self-help / Child Abuse

Cover illustration by Kirsten Walsh

Dear Reader

Thank you so much for reading my book.

This is a meaningful conversation we must have to enable change, and your presence here means more to me than I can express.

To support you as a reader of this story, I encourage you to take the time to reflect on and process what arises from your own experiences or those of someone close to you. This subject can be challenging and evoke feelings that resonate with your journey.

As you navigate the book, I want you to express whatever arises within you. I have provided a free downloadable workbook titled The Courage to Listen on my website to assist in this process. This resource is designed to accompany you as you read, offering gentle prompts and exercises to encourage self-reflection and expression.

If you feel triggered, or if particular sections bring up emotions you'd like to explore further, please use this workbook to navigate those feelings.

It's vital to check in with yourself: Are the stories you hold nurturing your growth or holding you back? Engaging with the prompts can help you process these internal dialogues, giving you the space to reframe your experiences in ways that support your healing journey and provide clarity to seek the help you need.

Be kind to yourself as you read.
Your experiences matter.
Thank you for joining me on this path of exploration and discovery.

With gratitude,
Kath

www.bespeak.au/book-bonus

Contents

A Poem of Thanks

To the women of strength, my family so dear,
Cousins, aunties, grandmothers – your love is so near.

To my mum, who stood firm through my moments of pain,
A guiding light when my thoughts felt unchained.
Though shadows fell heavy and I lost my way,
Know that I've freed every fragment of grey.

Now I'm stronger and wiser, and so are you,
Navigating this journey, we've made it on through.
With endless gratitude for all that you've done,
The clouds have now parted, and out comes the sun.

In my sister, my apprentice in parenting's embrace,
She gifted me joy – truly, my saving grace.
From sister to best friend, together we blend,
Thank you for loving me, right up to the end.

To my brother, so loyal, steadfast, and true,
Through life's winding paths, our hearts ever grew.
Your love and your kindness, a treasure so rare,
May it circle back to you, in abundance and care.

To my father, now gone, I forgive, and I see,
Your humour and heart were bright gifts gifted to me.
Though your journey ended with a heart steeped in pain,
May you find peace now, and be your own twin flame.

To my stepdad, taking me swimming every day.
And teaching me that retirement is just another way to play.
To the family I married into, being so safe and sound.
I am very grateful to the parents of the husband I found.

To friends from my school, lifelong and true,
A treasure of memories, both old and new.
My forever friends, through both joy and strife,
Your kindness and presence have often saved my life.

To new friends by the ocean, where we joyfully play,
This haven we've built will forever hold sway.
With bonds that won't falter, a circle so pure,
Together we flourish, together we endure.

To my daughter, my teacher, my heart's radiant spark,
In your dance and your laughter, you light up the dark.
Brave and so honest, you teach me each day,
The beauty that blossoms when love paves the way.

To my son, with compassion, a kindness so rare,
You're a beacon for change, with a heart full of care.
Determined and hardworking, a new strength to claim,
You'll show the world kindness is the way to win the game.

To my husband, my anchor, my partner, my guide,
You see all my colours, through the ebb and the tide.
Thank you for your love that stands steady and true,
Through every chapter of life, it's a journey with you.

Introduction

I have been blessed with the opportunity to heal, supported by a circle of kind individuals who have walked alongside me. Despite their best intentions, navigating the healing path has been excruciatingly lonely. It's a journey marked by the weight of hidden shame that only I could shift.

For too long, I have hidden not only from others but from myself, concealing the parts of my being that were wounded by an abuser. This loneliness can be stifling, and it drives home the reality that many share, often in silence. My intention for sharing my story is simple yet profound: to lessen that loneliness, to amplify the voices that yearn for connection, and to reach out to your inner child, who, like mine, seeks companionship and solace.

I trust that there are a variety of reasons this book finds its way into the hands of readers or the ears of listeners. If you are here to make sense of your own abuse, please let me begin by saying I am so deeply sorry that this happened to you. Your story is valid, and the journey towards healing is often fraught with challenges. If you are supporting a friend or relative as thcy grapple with their own resurfacing memories, thank you for being an ally.

I genuinely hope this book offers you insight into how you can best support them while also providing a space for you to process the emotions that may arise within yourself.

Trauma is multifaceted. First, I survived the abuse; then, I survived the resurfacing of those harrowing memories, followed by the mental health challenges that both events brought into my life. As I began to share my story more publicly, I encountered yet another layer – the challenge of vicarious trauma. Hearing the stories of others can be devastating, and throughout this journey, I have made every effort to be considerate of you, the reader, in an attempt to avoid further emotional distress.

The statistics surrounding childhood trauma are staggering, with 90 per cent of all child sexual abuse victims suffering at the hands of someone they trust[1] – a relative, a friend, a neighbour. As a mother, an aunt, and a friend to many children, I am driven by a deep desire to create a safer world for those who come after us. We must confront the generations of trauma and abuse that have perpetuated through silence. Only by breaking this silence can we begin to dismantle the walls dividing us and foster a profound sense of connection and healing.

Throughout my journey, writing has been my steadfast companion. The act of pouring my heart onto the page has allowed me to make sense of my feelings and memories, and it is through this medium that I hope to extend a hand to you. This book is not just a collection of my thoughts but rather a tapestry of short stories and poetry, woven together with the intention of enveloping you like a warm quilt – a quilt that hugs you tightly, reminding you that you are not alone. Together, these narratives are designed to foster understanding, empathy, and a sense of belonging.

As you turn these pages, I invite you to reflect on your own experiences and emotions. May my words inspire you to explore your own story, to find the tools that resonate with you, and to acknowledge the feelings that may have long been buried. Let this book serve as a bridge – a way for us all to connect deeply with one another and to our untold stories.

Throughout this process, I urge those of you who support others to prioritise your own wellbeing. Find your own support system; your oxygen mask must be nearby so that you can assist others in putting on theirs. By caring for yourself, you empower yourself to be the ally that others need during their healing journeys.

In our shared vulnerability, may we find strength, healing, and hope. Together, we can break the silence, create a supportive community, and pave the way for a future where it is more common for children to speak up than stay silent.

Chapter One

There was a girl who stayed silent, her voice not heard,
Yet within her, a world of thoughts and words.
Gregarious, friendly, a spirit bright and bold,
Busy, active, in her tales untold.
She never stopped talking, in her silent way,
Expressing through actions, each passing day.
A canvas of emotions, a heart that sings,
In her vibrant presence, the joy it brings.
Gregarious and open, a soul so free,
In her quiet strength, a symphony.
Though she didn't speak up, her essence shone bright,
A girl of many stories, in the softest light.

Flying

After enduring a long and turbulent flight from Melbourne to Perth, I reluctantly boarded the smaller plane bound for Karratha in the heart of Western Australia.

My heart pounded as I prepared to confront not one, but two, of my most paralysing fears.

The first was flying – a fear that had gripped me for as long as I could remember. Unlike in a car where I could see and often know the driver, flying left me in the hands of an unseen pilot. The vulnerability was unsettling, despite knowing that statistically, flying was safer than driving. My mind grappled with the unnerving fact that, thousands of metres above ground, we were at the mercy of fate and physics.

My thoughts raced. *Why did this fear of flying affect me so profoundly?* Were my trepidations rooted in the very nature of our flight – suspended mid-air, with the ground so far below that it seemed an abstract concept? Or was it the idea of relinquishing control to a person I couldn't see?

A good friend once told me, after I gained my driver's licence at 26, to drive as though everyone around me was on the brink of making a mistake. This principle of anticipating danger and closely assessing my surroundings had become second nature to me – a way of fostering a fragile sense of control and trust in an unpredictable world.

Yet here I was, thrust into a situation where the pilot remained a faceless entity, and my usual strategies to manage fear seemed useless.

Much like the unknown looming predator I had feared most of my life – the faceless man from my past – the pilot's anonymity added to my mounting anxiety. To make matters worse, I was the only woman on this flight, surrounded by older men whose lingering glances made my discomfort palpable.

Questions swirled in my mind. *Which one would I end up sitting next to? How could the flight attendants, outnumbered, maintain order if things went wrong? Was this an ominous preview of my new working environment? If my thoughts were already spiralling out of control, how could I possibly manage the upcoming 11 days?*

I envisioned myself alone, friendless, staying in a room by myself, and surrounded by men isolated from their families and responsibilities. The thought sent me further into a spiral, before the plane had even lifted off the tarmac.

Am I alone in my thinking? Do other people around me think this much, or is it just me?

I had barely slept the night before. Coupled with an early alarm and the fact that I was facing more uncertainty than I had experienced in a long time, my mind seemed incapable of relaxation. It was caught in a relentless cycle of anticipation and anxiety.

I lay there, eyes open, waiting for the alarm, petrified I'd oversleep and dreading the day ahead.

On this morning, the fatigue was more acute than ever. Emotionally drained, I grappled with the disappointment of missing a dear friend's wedding in Sydney because of this work trip. *Is this my new reality? Surrendering half of my social life to the ever-mounting pile of work commitments?*

I felt a pang of disconnect, as if I were losing the very threads that kept me connected to the joy and spontaneity of life. In addition to my exhaustion was another, deeper discomfort – the kind that settled in my bones and refused to leave.

It was the unease I felt around older men, especially when they encroached on my personal space. Once on the plane, this anxiety was heightened.

Surrounded by strangers and being the sole female in a plane full of men, the sensation of vulnerability was almost suffocating. My skin tingled with the type of unease I couldn't rationalise away.

To cope, I turned my attention to the view outside my window. The countryside sprawled below in a rich patchwork of red and brown, each hue blending seamlessly with the next. The tranquillity of the scene, coupled with the steady hum of the plane's engines, soothed my frazzled nerves. For a fleeting moment, I felt a sense of calm wash over me, easing my anxieties.

As the plane soared through the sky, carving its path towards our destination, I found myself humbled by the world's vastness. The complexity and diversity of the landscape reminded me of our smallness in this expansive universe. I took solace in pondering the mysteries of life, dwelling not on how things work, but on why they happen.

I had less interest in the mechanics of flight and was more intrigued by the reason for this plane being filled with this group of people. Was it a mere coincidence, or was there a deeper, more mystifying reason behind it?

To me, life had always felt like it held an undercurrent of magic, moments that seem too serendipitous to be random. I wondered if this flight, this job, and this journey were part of a grander narrative.

As my thoughts continued, the once steady flight turned into a bumpy rollercoaster ride. Each jolt brought my fears to life, circling around me like vultures, picking at my sense of insecurity. With every shake and shudder, doubts crept in, whispering insidious thoughts into my mind. Was the plane itself a threat, or was there someone on board I couldn't trust?

The turbulence intensified, and with it, my sense of vulnerability swelled. I was amidst rugged men, feeling more out of place than ever. My mind raced with questions, each one more unsettling than the last. *Was I truly prepared for this new job in the mining sector? Would I be able to cope with being so far from the family and friends I cherished and trusted? If something were to happen to me out here, who would even know?*

As my fears magnified, I realised there was nowhere to go, nowhere to escape. I glanced around the small cabin, my eyes landing on each of the men, all older than me. They exuded confidence and strength, qualities I was desperately trying to summon within myself.

While I was comfortable in the company of men my age, even relishing the easy camaraderie and occasional flirtation, older men made me uneasy. There was an inherent distrust and a bias that needed careful navigation within myself. My unease was only heightened by the fact that I was outnumbered.

As the doubts settled in my mind like unwelcome guests, I questioned my decision to accept this consulting contract. *Had I made a mistake? Was I really cut out for this line of work, or was I merely fooling myself into thinking I could handle it?* And the question that played on an endless loop in my head: ***Was I going to be safe?***

With each passing minute, my anxiety grew, and I grasped for any form of comfort I could find. The once-peaceful view outside the window was now tainted by the churning storm within me.

The chaos of my thoughts mirrored the turbulence of the plane, and I felt like a small bird caught in a relentless storm.

Was I going to be safe?

Like a fly you can't catch,
Coming back again to taunt you.
Inevitable
Unbearable
Fighting alone
The buzzing of your story in the dark.

Mantra

My resolve felt fragile, like it could shatter at any moment. I clutched my armrest, seeking solace in its solidity, trying to anchor myself amidst the swirling disturbance.

What else was there to grab onto in this moment? With my heart pounding and my breath shallow, I closed my eyes and clung to a mantra that had become a lifeline in times of distress. I silently repeated it over and over in my mind, hoping it would calm my racing thoughts and soothe my frayed nerves: *I am strong, I am safe, I am protected, and I am guided.*

Each repetition served as a quiet affirmation, a whispered reminder that I had the strength within me to face any challenge, no matter how daunting.

These words were my anchor, giving me the courage to open my eyes and confront the situation head-on.

This mantra wasn't just a series of words; it was my guiding light in moments when I felt lost and alone. On this turbulent plane, it was my constant companion, providing a comforting sense of security and inner strength.

I am strong, I am safe, I am protected, I am guided.

The cadence of these words became a shield, insulating me from the chaos both within and around me. They helped me project an air of composure, an external illusion that matched the confidence of the men surrounding me.

Even as my insides churned with doubt and fear, the mantra helped me forge a veneer of calm.

In that small, confined cabin, my mantra sat alongside me like an invisible friend – the only friend I felt I had in that moment. It drowned out the childlike voices in my head that were pleading with me to listen, to heed their fears and anxieties.

I am strong, I am safe, I am protected, I am guided.

This refrain seemed to emanate from both within and outside of me simultaneously, as though it was an intrinsic part of my being, but also a gift from something greater. It felt powerful, certain, and convincing – almost as if it was a message from a future self, reassuring the present me that I had the fortitude to endure.

In that turbulent flight, amidst strangers and insecurities, these words were my sanctuary. They enveloped me in a cocoon of self-belief, urging me to hold on just a little longer, to believe in my resilience. It was in this inner sanctum of repeated assurance that I found the strength to persevere, even when everything else seemed uncertain.

It was the only truth I had – the single belief that made me feel I could reach deep inside myself and find the confidence to step off that plane and succeed in one of the most male-dominated work environments in Australia.

I am Strong,
I am Safe,
I am Protected,
I am Guided.

In the face of fear, I stand tall,
For I am strong, I will not fall.
With every step, I am safe,
In the warmth of love, I find my place.

Protected by a higher power above,
Guided by wisdom, faith, and love.
I move forward with courage and grace,
Embracing challenges that I face.

No storm can shake my inner core,
For I am strong, now and forevermore.
Safe within my own embrace,
Protected, guided by a divine grace.

Red Soil

The plane landed in Karratha, a town in Western Australia renowned for its hot, luminous days. The sun's rays danced upon the crystalline waters of the bay, creating a dazzling display of light. The dusty red paths and expansive stretches of land adorned with resilient trees and hardy shrubs offered a breathtaking sight, a stark contrast to the familiar greenery of Melbourne where I grew up.

The mining industry cast a long shadow over the Pilbara, with its endless, windy roads and the omnipresent dust swirling in the air. The constant hum of heavy machinery and the occasional thunderous blasts were a testament to the bustling activity within the mines.

The demand for iron ore was so high that ships were constantly rotating, each waiting their turn to load their valuable cargo. All these vessels came from China, ready to carry a commodity that was initially a mystery to me – I didn't even know the difference between iron and iron ore. How was I supposed to excel in this job when I didn't grasp the basic aspects of the trade?

But soon, I grasped that iron ore is the raw material extracted from the earth, rich in iron oxides, and people refine it to get pure iron, a fundamental element for steel production. Essentially, China was buying up vast quantities so they could construct extensively with the resulting steel.

Despite the harshness of the environment, the town exuded a unique, rustic charm, with its towering industrial structures standing tall against the expansive blue sky.

As I stepped off the plane, a colleague – a good man who had recommended me for this job, greeted me. His familiar presence made me feel a little less alone amidst the unfamiliar surroundings. He knew this world inside-out, as intimately as I knew the shop layouts in Chadstone. To me, it felt as foreign as an overseas land, so far removed from the language and culture I had known.

The conversations here, revolving around the Aboriginal communities, were a far cry from the equal opportunity issues we debated at the dinner table back in Bayside Melbourne. The lack of female presence was a stark contrast to the empowering atmosphere of my Catholic girls' school, which proudly counted Germaine Greer among its alumni.

The rallying cry of "We are women, hear us roar" now morphed into a quieter, more desperate plea: "I am a woman, can you hear my internal scream?" The empowering chants of my inner feminist seemed to echo hollowly in this rugged, male-dominated landscape.

In those initial moments, the mantra that had sustained me during the flight returned with renewed vigour.

I am strong, I am safe, I am protected, I am guided.

These words, my unyielding truth, reminded me I had the strength within to navigate this unknown terrain. I clung to them as I would to a lifeline, using them to bolster my courage. With each step, I reminded myself that I had earned the selection for this role for a reason. There was something that had brought me to this place. As much as I felt like an outsider in a world dominated by rugged men and heavy machinery, I knew that my presence here was an opportunity for learning and growth.

The stark beauty of Dampier, the mining city I'd be working in, 20kms from Karratha, worked its way into my bones. It was a land that demanded respect, one that would challenge anyone who dared to work within it. I couldn't help but feel admiration for those who called this place their home, who thrived amidst such unforgiving conditions.

The colleague who picked me up drove us through the town, pointing out landmarks and sharing snippets of local history. His familiarity with the place was comforting; his stories offered me a glimpse into the community and its complexities. He spoke of the shift schedules, the camaraderie among workers, and the unspoken rules of respect and resilience that governed life here in the Pilbara.

That evening, as the sun set and cast a golden glow over the red earth, I stood at the window of my work, looking out at the vast landscape. The mantra that had carried me thus far echoed in my mind. *I am strong, I am safe, I am protected, I am guided.*

In the solitude of that moment, I made a silent vow to myself. I would face this new chapter with the same strength and determination that had brought me here. I would carve out my place in this male-dominated environment, proving not only to myself but to everyone else that I could succeed.

Alone in the depths of the earth, I toil,
A woman in a world of dust and soil.
Alone in the depths of the earth to roam,
Isolated from friends and family back home.
Each day a struggle, a battle to survive,
Fear and vulnerability my constant drive.
Surrounded by perceived danger, my heart afraid,
In this desolate place, my spirit swayed.
The weight of isolation heavy on my soul,
In this harsh environment, it takes its toll.
But in this challenge, a rare sight,
Hope and courage shining bright.
I find strength within, a fire ignited,
Through the challenges faced, I'm delighted.
For in the mines, though isolated and alone,
I find resilience and a spirit of my own.

Shelter

As I arrived at my accommodation, all my fears resurfaced with a vengeance. The donga, a small and rundown accommodation in the heart of a deserted town, greeted me with an unsettling silence. It reminded me of old school portables, lined up one after the other.

The term 'donga' is used in Australia to refer to temporary or transportable accommodation units typically used in mining camps or construction sites. The origin of the word in an Australian context is not definitively known, but it is believed to have originated from either the United States or the United Kingdom.

One theory is that the term originated in the United States as a slang term for a special type of house or cabin that could be easily transported or moved. Another theory suggests that it may have evolved from the British slang term 'dong' which refers to a narrow alleyway or passage.

Regardless of its origins, the term 'donga' has become a common part of Australian mining lingo, used to describe accommodation units that are often simple and basic in design.

In the context of mining communities, the term may have been used to indicate that the accommodation was intended for female residents or families of higher social status or those associated with the mining company's management or administration.

It could also reflect the cultural norms and social hierarchies that existed in these mining communities.

Ironically, I could stay the night at Crown Towers for less than this was costing Rio Tinto for having me stay here each night!

The quiet that enveloped the accommodation only added to the eerie atmosphere of the donga, intensifying my sense of isolation. It was a place that I dreaded returning to each day, yet I had no other option.

I remember one night when the fear and loneliness felt almost unbearable. Only the relentless beating of my heart broke the oppressive silence, echoing through the empty room. The darkness seemed to swallow me whole, leaving me huddled in a corner, desperately searching for some semblance of comfort. But there was none to be found.

It reminded me of my childhood, when I slept in my cupboard the first night my stepdad stayed over for the night. Not sure if I was safe, I chose to ensure I was by hiding there until the light of the morning peeked through the window. It didn't take me long to realise I was indeed safe in my stepdad's company. I didn't realise that was an odd response for an eight-year-old until adulthood.

The donga was the starkest contrast imaginable to the bustling, lively atmosphere of my workplace. Each evening, as I returned to that dreary accommodation, my mantra became a lifeline, its repetitive reassurance the only thing keeping me grounded.

I am strong, I am safe, I am protected, I am guided.

These words played on an endless loop in my mind, and I believe they saved me from slipping into despair.

Realising the psychological toll the donga was taking on me, I approached one of my mentors with a request. I asked if I could move, at least on the weekends, to the accommodation where all the university students were staying together. The thought of being closer to a vibrant community, even if only temporarily, offered a flicker of hope. To my relief, they approved the move.

Each weekend, I left the desolation of the donga and headed to the lively quarters brimming with students.

My routine became one of work by day, and in the evening, retreating to my room to watch episodes of *Sex and the City* or a host of other female-dominated romcoms or documentaries.

The noise from the student parties outside was oddly comforting. It felt honest, familiar, and real – a chaotic symphony of youth.

Arriving at the donga, fears emerge,
Silence and unease, a dreary surge.
In a deserted town, rundown and stark,
Reminiscent of old school portables, in the dark.

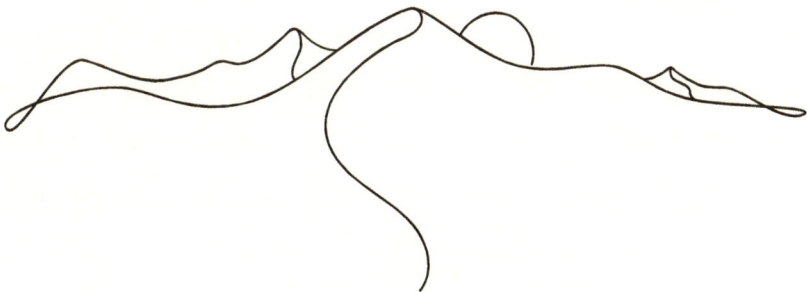

Alone

There wasn't much in Dampier where I stayed — just a pub, a bottle shop, and a milk bar. The limited amenities underscored the isolation of mining life. The pub, while certainly not offering the finest wine, served as a sort of refuge from the harshness outside.

As we sipped our overpriced drinks and ate our $65 steak, the sounds of lively chatter and laughter from the bar next door drifted over, a stark reminder of company and camaraderie that seemed just beyond reach. I often wondered about the young female backpackers working in that bar, serving drinks to a room full of men undoubtedly ogling their exposed breasts. *If only my friends back home, leisurely sipping gin and tonics, could see me now*, I thought.

I never ventured into that bar, despite the fleeting temptation to do so for the sake of shock value. Back home, in the safety of my seaside haven, I joked with friends about the idea. Perhaps with a female friend by my side, I might have ventured in, allowing my alter ego Katarina to mock and judge the scene. But I didn't feel safe or strong enough to step foot in that place by myself. My inner guidance insisted I stay away, warning me to steer clear of anyone lurking within those walls.

The attention I received merely for being a young, healthy woman in a predominantly male environment was more than enough. Listening to that inner voice had protected me before. It was the same instinct that prompted me to seek refuge in a stranger's house when a car full of men slowed to follow me during a lunchtime run. It was the same voice that told me to wait for my male colleagues to leave breakfast with me at 5:30 am, while a man who had been drinking all night watched us from afar.

This inner voice also guided me back to sleep when sudden noises woke me, often just a kangaroo passing through the grounds – or at least that is what I told myself.

Nights were the hardest, the time when my vulnerability felt most acute. I took to wearing clothes to bed instead of pyjamas, ready to flee or fight if necessary. Not every night, but on those especially lonely weekends in the donga, the precaution felt necessary. *How long could I endure this?*

I worked in Dampier for 18 months, and during that time, the pressing sense of isolation was a heavy burden that weighed on me. Weekends were challenging, and without the company and camaraderie of my colleagues, the solitude became unbearable.

Each time I found myself alone, I would call my boyfriend in tears, confiding that I was at my wit's end, desperate to return home. I would tell him it was simply too much to bear. Each time, he would patiently reassure me that it would all be okay and that we could talk things through when I visited home. His support was a lifeline during those dark moments.

Once back in the comforting embrace of my coastal home, the agony of isolation would fade into a distant memory. It's almost like my brain shielded me from the true intensity of the isolation. The comfort and familiarity of home gave me the strength to head back to Dampier, restarting the cycle all over again.

At work, I was fortunate to be surrounded by some excellent colleagues. The men I worked with made me feel safe and took care of me like a younger sister. They provided a sense of belonging that was incredibly vital in such a remote location. Moreover, the consultants who travelled from Perth appreciated the personal connections I made with them. They genuinely valued my interest in their families. When I remembered important details, such as a grandson's important football match or a wife's birthday party, it fostered a sense of gratitude and camaraderie.

Coming from Melbourne meant I stayed for 11 days straight before getting a 10-day break. On paper, this arrangement seemed ideal – an extended period off after a stretch of workdays. However, the reality was far from dreamy. The constant flights and long workdays left me physically and emotionally drained. I spent most of my time at home, which should have been for rest and recovery, trying to recuperate in a place where I felt truly secure.

The cycle of flights and exhaustive work had taken its toll, leaving me in a perpetual state of fear and unrest. Even at home, where I had hoped to find solace, I would find myself on edge, constantly looking over my shoulder, and becoming startled by the smallest noises. Instead of enjoying my time off, anxiety and hypervigilance trapped me in a loop.

The cycle continued for 18 long months: separation-induced anxiety, emotional breakdowns over the phone, a brief respite at home, and then the reluctant return to Dampier.

Reflecting on this time, I realise the resilience I built in myself and the profound importance of the human connections I formed. Those bonds, coupled with the support of my boyfriend, were my anchors.

It reminded me of a story I had read, about how there really is no shortcut to building strength. It was about a young boy who came across a butterfly cocoon and brought it into his house. He watched, over the course of hours, as the butterfly struggled to break free from its confinement. It managed to create a small hole in the cocoon, but its body was too large to emerge. It was tired and became still.

Wanting to help the butterfly, the boy snipped a slit in the cocoon with a pair of scissors. But the butterfly was small, weak, and its wings crumpled. The boy expected the insect to take flight, but instead it could only drag its undeveloped body along the ground. It was incapable of flying.

The boy, in his eagerness to help the butterfly, stunted its development. What he did not know was that the butterfly needed to go through the process of struggling against the cocoon to gain strength and fill its wings with blood. It was the struggle that made the wings stronger.

Aloneness wasn't a new feeling. I had felt this way before, as a child, but back then, this comforting mantra wasn't there to guide me. When I was a child, confusion and fear enshrouded me like a haze. I lacked the words to articulate the bewildering experiences unfolding around me. There was an overwhelming sense that I had no control over my life. I was just a small, frightened figure in a vast, unpredictable world.

As a child, emotions coursed through me – fear, sadness, anxiety – but I didn't have the tools to express them or the understanding to voice my concerns. This internal disarray left me feeling utterly powerless, unable to take flight, much like the butterfly.

People around me were unaware of the silent turmoil that churned within me. They couldn't see the danger that lurked around me, and therefore, they couldn't protect me. I had to navigate the chaotic and often frightening labyrinth of my childhood on my own.

There were moments, many moments, where I longed for someone to tell me that everything would be okay, to offer a gentle reassurance that could subdue my fears. But that comforting presence was absent. I had to rely on whatever inner strength I could muster, a child trying to build armour out of innocence and confusion.

I remember feeling alone, despite being surrounded by a loving family. I gravitated towards minor comforts, unnoticed by others – an imaginary world, filled with fairies and angels that were with me always. It was not until I became an adult that I realised how critical those intangible beliefs were in helping me survive my loneliness as a child.

I grew up forced to grapple with these unnamed fears, and without the words to describe them, they remained shadows in my young mind. This confusion and fear hardened into a quiet resolve over the years, shaping me in ways I only understood much later. I knew I was scared, but I didn't know specifically what I was fearing, just like how I felt as an adult in Dampier.

My adult self was still deeply triggered by childhood experiences that I was still yet to make complete sense of.

Each stimulus triggers the lost little girl inside,
Cautious and vigilant, seeking a place to confide.
But a mantra appears so she's not alone,
Words emulating strength deep inside her bones.
Being in tune, embracing her inner glow,
Supporting her as she perseveres and grows.
Trusting in the process, embracing her gut,
The journey moulding her lost self out of this rut.
Every trigger awakens the lost little girl within,
Watchful and wary, the journey of healing begins.

Aim to Please

From a young age, I discovered the ease of relating to people. It wasn't just a skill I developed; it was a lifeline. This ability to connect with others kept me safe, alert, and aware. Navigating the complexities of human interactions became second nature to me, almost like a dance I instinctively knew the steps too. I was that happy, funny, and lively child who had a knack for making people smile.

I was often the oldest child in the room, so I learnt to watch adults speak to each other, and observe them in their interactions. I quickly learnt when to speak and how to speak to them so they would listen. I could just as skilfully be invisible as I could contribute to the conversation.

Adults would often comment on how I was so wise for my age, and I cherished their praise, basking in the glow of their affection. But my charm wasn't solely for attention; it was also my shield. By pleasing others, I created an environment where I felt secure.

The smiles and laughter I elicited built a fortress around me, warding off any negativity that might seep through. My keen sense of awareness helped me read moods and adapt my behaviour, ensuring harmony wherever I went.

One of my greatest gifts was my imagination. It allowed me to fill in the gaps during quiet moments and transform the mundane into magical. I could turn a simple afternoon in the backyard into a grand adventure as a mermaid or fairy, with hidden treasures and daring quests. My imagination, my trusted companion, always stood ready to transport me to a world where everything was possible, and safety was guaranteed.

In the classroom, my engaging stories and quick wit made me a favourite among peers. I could see when someone was feeling down, and with a few kind words or a funny anecdote, I could lift their spirits. My teachers appreciated my eagerness to help and my easy rapport with other students. They often relied on me to smooth over social rough patches, knowing my natural charm could diffuse tension.

My ability to connect with others also forged deep and lasting friendships. My friends knew they could count on me for a good laugh, a comforting word, or a shoulder to cry on. I was the one who remembered birthdays, who knew just the right thing to say, and who always made time for everyone. My relationships were a tapestry woven with threads of kindness, empathy, and joy, and I took immense pride in the happiness I brought to those around me.

My knack for pleasing others was both my gift and my refuge. Amidst life's uncertainties, it was the one thing I could control. I found solace knowing that, through my interactions, I made the world a little brighter. The endless well of my imagination complemented my social interactions, adding layers of creativity and spontaneity that enchanted those I encountered.

Even in solitude, my imagination thrived. I would play make-believe games, crafting elaborate narratives that kept me entertained and content. Lost in these daydreams, I could be anyone, go anywhere, and do anything, all from the safety of my little corner of the world. The stories I created in my mind were so vivid, it felt like I was living a thousand lives.

As I grew older, the skills I honed as a child became the foundation of my relationships and interactions. The empathy, awareness, and creativity that defined my early years continued to serve me well into adulthood. These attributes not only helped me navigate social landscapes, but also allowed me to forge meaningful and enduring connections.

Looking back, I realise how being a happy little people pleaser wasn't just about avoiding conflict or gaining approval; it was about control and safety. If I had people around, I was safe. *Stay with everyone else and he can't get to you.*

I still carry that same sense of wonder and love for people. I continue to draw on my imagination to keep things fresh and engaging, and my social ease ensures that I remain a bridge-builder in any community I'm part of.

This included the world I found myself in at Dampier. As I stood on the precipice of my isolated work environment, questions lingered in my mind, gnawing at the edges of my consciousness.

Why was I here?

Which lessons did I need to learn?

What foundations was this period of my life laying for me?

I couldn't shake the feeling that this experience held a unique opportunity for growth, an opportunity that could only manifest in these challenging circumstances. It was as if the universe had conspired to place me here, not as a punishment, but to forge a stronger, more resilient version of myself.

From youth, finding solace in connections deep,
Navigating interactions, a dance to keep,
Observing, learning from adults wise,
Creating positive spaces, charm as a guise.

Imagination's magic, turning mundane to bright,
Engaging, lifting spirits with tales in flight,
Deep friendships woven, in kindness and care,
A tapestry of joy that we share.

Pleasing others, a gift and shield,
Crafting stories in solitude's yield,
Empathy, creativity sown since youth,
Guiding me through life's honest truth.

Home

Deep down, I sensed there was something here for me to conquer: fears to face, strength to gather, a voice to find. Perhaps I needed to confront my own biases, to cast aside preconceived notions and emerge with a clearer, more open perspective.

Each lonely weekend, every tearful phone call to my boyfriend, and all the moments of inner turmoil seemed to chisel away at my outer shell, revealing the core of who I truly was beneath the surface.

Reflecting on my past, I couldn't help but notice the constant movement that defined my early adulthood. From the age of 18 to 28, I had never stayed in one place for very long. Each year brought about a new abode. It was exhilarating yet exhausting.

Now back in Victoria, here I was, embarking on a new chapter of my life as a grown-up, in a house that was owned by my boyfriend. It made me pause and question everything.

Is this the place where I was supposed to settle down?

Was he the one I was to build a future with?

Was this the town I wanted to call home?

I realised that my nomadic lifestyle had served its purpose, allowing me to explore a variety of places by not standing still and always being surrounded by people. This made me feel safe. But now, as I stood on the brink of a more stable, rooted existence, I couldn't help but wonder if I was ready to stand still?

Only time would tell if this house would become our home, if my boyfriend was truly the one I wanted to share my life with, if this town held the potential for a fulfilling future.

For now, I allowed myself to embrace the uncertainty, knowing that every new chapter brings both challenges and opportunities. I felt like the isolation and time working on my own in Dampier was a challenge I had to overcome before being gifted with the opportunity for a serene seaside life.

The struggle, the isolation, the fear – they were all part of the gauntlet I had to run. I needed to prove to myself that I could endure, adapt, and thrive on my own before committing to life with someone else. For the first time since my childhood, I learnt to keep my own company, finding solace within myself.

It was a revelation to realise that, even in the depths of isolation, I could be my own source of company and comfort. With my inner compass guiding me, I resolved to take each day as it came, to extract every lesson, and to build the strongest foundations I could from this experience, both professionally and personally.

If this chapter was a test, I intended to pass with flying colours, knowing that on the other side awaited the life I yearned for – one shaped by the trials I overcame and the strength I discovered within myself.

With a renewed resolve and my mantra lighting the way, I took a deep breath. Knowing I was ready to face whatever came next on my own, allowed me to confirm my life with this boyfriend who would become my husband. A man who had already seen the worse of me. A man that knew my fears. A man that understood my story was held in my body and the depth of my soul more than anyone else could.

Each challenge I faced held the promise of transformation. I was no longer alone in the belief that I had the strength to forge a path not just to survive, but to truly thrive. He also became a mirror that reflected this back to me, today and many times when I stumbled into the future.

Home is safe, or so they say,
But sometimes doubt gets in the way.
Is solace found within these walls,
Or is it just a fleeting call?
A place to regroup, to find my peace,
But can I truly let worries cease?
Happiness lingers, yet so does doubt,
Loneliness whispers without a shout.
Home, a haven or a cage,
Where fears and joys engage.
A paradox, a blend of light and shade,
Where loneliness is quietly laid.

Chapter Two

The March

In 2021, as a mother of a six-year-old son and a ten-year-old daughter, I noticed the stirring currents of societal change. A significant focus in the media on the inequality and mistreatment of women marked the year, igniting a firestorm of discourse across the globe.

We bore witness to the extraordinary courage of women like Grace Tame and Brittany Higgins, who bravely stepped forward to share their harrowing experiences of sexual assault. These women, among others, have become symbols of hope and change. Through their stories, they shed light on the culture of silence and enabling that perpetuates such injustices.

As I watched these stories unfold, I felt a swell of anger and frustration bubbling inside me. My heart ached for these women, for all women who have experienced mistreatment, silence, and dismissal. Their bravery highlighted the persistent lack of systemic change, and I couldn't help but see the reflection of my strength in their resolve. The frustration I felt grew daily, and I knew I had to act – not just for myself, but for my children.

The tipping point came when I attended a protest march with my children. There was an urgency to be part of the collective voice demanding justice. I wanted my children to understand the importance of standing up for what is right, to witness firsthand the power of solidarity, and to know that genuine change requires action.

Hundreds of like-minded individuals gathered, our shared purpose creating a palpable energy that pulsed through the crowd. My children, wide-eyed and curious, held my hands as we navigated through streams of people.

The culmination of the protest was an awe-inspiring moment. We stood on the beach, surrounded by members of our community, and watched as volunteers meticulously arranged their bodies to form the word 'JUSTICE' on the sand. It was a powerful visual statement – a testament to our collective yearning for change. Subsequently, they took an aerial shot and shared the photo all over the Australian media.

My children looked on; their youthful faces marked by contemplation. My daughter squeezed my hand, and my son looked up at me with a mix of confusion and newfound understanding. I knelt at their level, imparting the importance of what they were witnessing. This wasn't just a protest; it was a movement, a promise to make the world a fairer place for them and future generations.

As a mother, I felt a renewed sense of purpose. Witnessing the bravery of those who spoke out during the #MeToo movement and feeling the energy from the protest march, I became determined to be an active participant in driving change.

The questions that lingered in 2021, both in the broader societal context and within my journey, remained ever relevant.

Why was this happening?

What lessons were we, as a society, supposed to learn?

What kind of foundation were we laying for future generations?

I felt it was my duty as a mother to both protect and empower my children. This meant equipping them with the knowledge and values to create a fair world. By taking them to the protest, I hoped to ingrain in them the understanding that fighting for justice and standing against oppression is a responsibility we all share.

On the sandy shores, just another day,
We march for justice, united in what we say.
The waves crash, a symbol of our strength,
United in purpose, we will go to any length.
Justice is the focus, that is why we are here,
Standing strong, our message is clear.

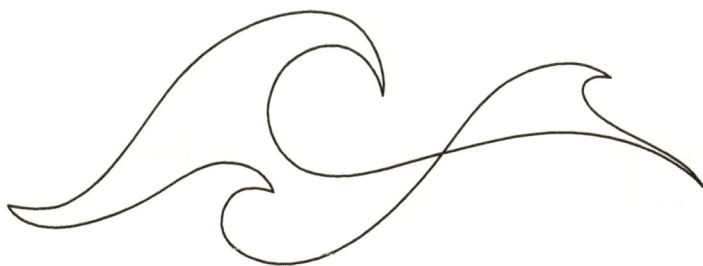

Objective Viewpoint

As the protest dispersed, the image of 'JUSTICE' lingered in my mind. It was more than just a word; it was a sign to keep pushing forward. And just as my mantra became my personal guiding light, it also served as a beacon for our community, reminding us of the importance of perseverance and collective action.

Amid the swirling tides of change, I found myself blessed with an objective viewpoint, particularly for the welfare and upbringing of my children. The responsibilities I shouldered as their mother and guide felt both monumental and profoundly grounding. Each day, I strived to instill values that would equip them to navigate a world. Each day I looked at the world through two lenses.

How will this affect my daughter?

How will this affect my son?

I was at this march because I aspired to bring up a son who embraced kindness, empathy, and awareness. I wanted him to grow into a man who would embody these principles in his interactions with the world. I wanted him to be aware of the issues surrounding the safety of his sister, mother, and friends. It was essential that he grasp the importance of consent and respect, recognising that these were not just abstract concepts, but vital components of everyday interactions.

Teaching him to be kind was the cornerstone of this endeavour. Kindness, in its truest form, is an active force. It requires awareness, understanding, and a willingness to stand up against injustices, no matter how small. My guidance aimed to nurture these qualities in him, enabling him to become an ally and advocate across all communities.

I was also there because I needed my daughter to know that she deserves to feel safe, valued, and empowered. The courage of women like Grace Tame and Brittany Higgins served as powerful examples for her. It was imperative that she understood her worth and felt confident in her right to be heard. My desire was for her to believe in the importance of her voice and recognise that speaking out against injustice was not only her right but also her responsibility, both for herself and to those who she knows that may struggle to find their own voices along the way.

The focus for my daughter's safety is not just about protection from physical harm. It is about creating an environment where she feels emotionally secure and empowered to express herself freely. It was about eradicating the fear that has silenced so many women before her, myself included.

At 11, I began this conversation by focusing on her friendships.

"How does that friend make you feel?" I would ask her. My mission was to instill a sense of unshakeable self-worth, encouraging her to stand tall and to understand she had a choice to advocate for herself.

As I look at consent and the potential challenges my children will face in their teenage years and beyond, I find myself gifted with a viewpoint of heightened awareness. I have no choice but to look at consent through the lenses of girls and boys. How can I educate my daughter to stand up for herself? How can I educate my son to understand the needs of the person he is with and not step over that line?

For my children's growth, my deepest desire is for them to grow into individuals who are both emotionally intelligent and respectful of others. Teaching them to be aware of and articulate their own emotions is, I believe, fundamental to achieving this goal.

Discussing the concept of personal space and boundaries explicitly with my children is another vital aspect of their education. I clarify that everyone has the right to their own personal space and the right to feel comfortable within it. This conversation is ongoing and aims to reinforce the importance of respecting boundaries – both their own and those of others.

I explain to them that understanding and respecting personal space is a fundamental aspect of healthy relationships. It's about understanding that it's okay to say "no" and that others should respect their "no". Conversely, it's equally important for them to recognise and honour the boundaries set by their friends and peers.

Since Covid, anxiety in children has been elevated, we have had many children come to have a sleepover, only to change their mind before the sleep arrives. I love that these children feel comfortable enough to share with me how they are feeling and have the confidence to express it.

This was not encouraged when I was a child – we were 'good' if we were compliant. This didn't serve me, and I will not instill the same belief in my children or the children who are in our world. Be respectful of the home you are visiting, yes, but that doesn't mean not trusting your own feelings or that you are not allowed to change your mind about what you thought you wanted. If children are not taught this, how can we expect our teenagers to navigate the same concept when they are exploring more complex learnings around consent?

Through these conversations, I aim to empower my children with the confidence to advocate for themselves, ensuring they feel secure and valued. More importantly, I want them to grow up respecting the autonomy and individuality of others, understanding that every person deserves to feel safe and respected in their own space. I soon learnt that this teaching didn't extend very far from our home.

Teaching children to voice their needs,
Respecting boundaries, planting a valuable seed.
To listen and understand, when "no" is the reply,
Empowering them with a voice, not to comply.
Consent is the key, to honour and uphold,
In a world where respect and understanding mould.
To acknowledge and respect each other's right,
Creating a culture of safety and light.
Let children know their worth, we are listening near.
Empowering them to speak up, without fear.
Teaching the value of consent, from the start,
Building a foundation of respect and heart.

Boys will be Boys

During a parent-teacher interview, I expressed my concern about some of the behaviour my daughter had observed among the boys in the playground. The teacher's response was, "boys will be boys". Under the table, my husband tightened his grip on my hand, steadying me and acknowledging that he, too, found the comment disturbing. I realised that addressing my concerns here would be futile.

The following day, I attended a parent information night about the upcoming grade five and six puberty sessions. Determined to address the issue, I repeatedly asked, "Do you cover respectful behaviour? Do you teach what is appropriate?" Each time, the response was a confident "Yes, of course."

However, I pushed further. "Do you explain to the boys that pretending to masturbate and threatening to spray others with 'their father's milk' is unacceptable?" The room fell silent, jaws dropped.

Now, I had their attention.

After the session, two female teachers approached me. They assured me that if such incidents happened again, the school needed to be informed immediately. I agreed but pointed out, "During a parent-teacher interview, the teacher had dismissed me with 'boys will be boys'."

I don't want my daughter subjected to that, nor do I want my son or his friends to think they can get away with it; they all deserve better.

Thankfully, the other teachers that my children have had so far, both male and female, have been incredible. I am so grateful that so many positive messages are now being shared through our education system. I just hope these teachers are gifted with the additional support and opportunities for education to continue to grow, so that they are equipped to navigate the very messy social learnings that children have during these formative vulnerable years.

"Boys will be boys", a saying often heard,
Excusing behaviour, with harmful words.
But this attitude, it's not okay,
In shaping our sons, a different way.

For I want my son to understand,
Respect for all, hand in hand.
To know that kindness, is the key,
A good human, how he should be.

Not bound by stereotypes, old and untrue,
But free to express, in all he'll pursue.
To treat others with care and respect,
In words and actions, to reflect.

So, let's break free from outdated norms,
And teach our sons, from life's storms,
That goodness and empathy, they should embrace,
In their hearts, let these virtues find their place.

Good Men

In my life, like the teachers who have guided my kids, I have been fortunate to be exposed to an array of positive influence from both women and men, both in my professional and personal life. I consider myself incredibly lucky because I know what a good man is.

My stepdad, for instance, has been a calm and intelligent presence in my life, never once raising his voice at me. His patience and wisdom have been pillars of support, providing a safe and nurturing environment in which I could grow and thrive.

Then there are my uncles who embody kindness and empathy. These good men have treated me with respect and understanding, their actions speaking louder than any words could. Their warmth and compassion during my upbringing reinforced my belief in the goodness of people and showed me a healthy way to demonstrate masculinity.

More recently, I have seen the same qualities in my husband and father-in-law, who are funny, compassionate, hardworking and kind. My son is lucky to have these men in his orbit, guiding him to who he will become.

All these men have shown me the importance of emotional intelligence and gentle strength.

They have been living examples of how to treat others with kindness and respect, regardless of the circumstances. Through them, I've learnt that true strength lies in patience, understanding, and the ability to inspire trust and loyalty in those around us.

Knowing such good men has deeply influenced my perspective on relationships and the qualities I value in others. They've set a high standard, showing that masculinity can coexist with gentleness, that authority doesn't require aggression, and that empathy and love are the foundations of true power.

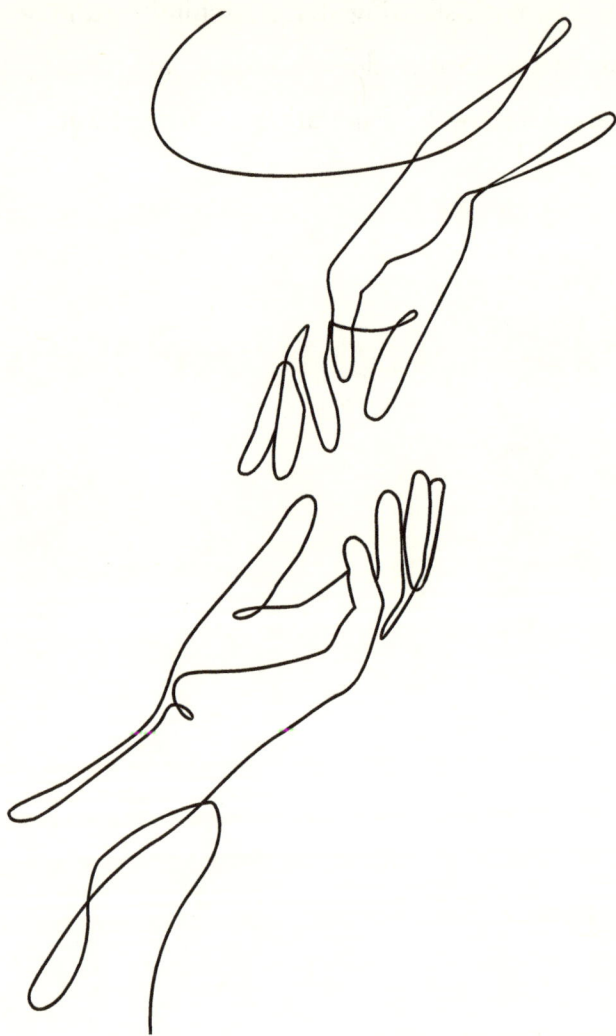

In a world where power beckons, attention calls,
Love sought in ways that build walls.
But how do we shift this generation's course,
Help them resist, find a different source?

To show that strength lies in lifting others high,
In lending a hand, in reaching for the sky.
A good man, not defined by power or fame,
But by kindness, by actions that proclaim,

That true strength is found in humility,
In compassion and empathy's dexterity.
To set aside ego, to listen and understand,
To uplift, to support, to lend a helping hand.

So let us teach our sons this vital truth,
That goodness and kindness are the ultimate booth.
In a world that craves power and might,
A good man shines brightest, in love's pure light.

Strong Women

The strong women in my life have had a profound impact on shaping who I am today. I am grateful for their presence. My mother stands out prominently among them. She dedicated her career to social justice, tackling inequalities and fighting for the disenfranchised with a fervent determination that often took more from her than she should have allowed.

Yet, despite the sacrifices and the emotional toll, my mum's unwavering commitment to her cause has always inspired me deeply. Her career was more than a job; it was a calling, a purpose woven into the very fabric of who she is. Watching her navigate the complexities and challenges of fighting for social justice exposed me to the stark realities many face, especially in terms of socio-economic disparities.

She did more than pave a way to creating change – she laid down a blueprint for me to follow. Her work illuminated the systemic inequalities that exist in society, demonstrating to me just how deep and pervasive these issues are.

She first educated me about the struggles of families battling poverty, the barriers faced by marginalised communities, and the critical importance of advocacy and policy change.

Her dedication served as a powerful lesson in resilience and perseverance. She showed me that true strength lies not in avoiding the tough battles but in confronting them head-on, even when the personal cost is high. My mum's career, though taxing, was a testament to the impact one can make through relentless effort and passionate advocacy.

Growing up with such a role model has profoundly shaped my values and aspirations. I learnt the importance of empathy, the necessity of standing up for what is right, and the power of using one's voice to effect change. My mother's career made me deeply aware of my privileges and the responsibility to use them for uplifting others and addressing inequities.

Witnessing her father's experiences with discrimination as his condition, Friedrich's ataxia, gradually confined him to a wheelchair profoundly shaped my mother's sense of justice. She once recounted a time when they went to test drive a car that required special attachments on the steering wheel for her father to use. The salesman never acknowledged my grandfather, speaking only to my mother, as if he were incapable of participating in the conversation. These experiences fuelled my mother's determination to advocate for justice and fairness, having seen firsthand the bias and judgement her father endured.

My brother, sister and I were frequently involved in discussions about my mother's work challenges. I have a vivid memory of her advocating for a transgender employee who was being forced to use the disabled toilet. The workplace failed to understand the profound impact this had on the individual. This was over 30 years ago.

At the time, I was unaware that these conversations were not normal for family dinners. It wasn't until I moved away that I realised our differing understandings of equality. I am grateful for the education that I received.

My mother's dedication to justice has inspired and equipped me to contribute to the ongoing fight for social justice. Her strength, tenacity, and unwavering belief in the power of change are gifts I cherish and aim to embody in everything I do.

As I stood after the protest had dispersed, the image of "JUSTICE" lingered in my mind. It was more than a word; it was an urgent call to keep pushing forward.

In the presence of strong women, I stand tall,
Their impact on me, profound overall.
Among them, my mother shines bright,
A beacon of justice, a guiding light.

Her career a dedication to right the wrongs,
Fighting for the disenfranchised, where she belongs.
Through sacrifices and emotional strain,
Her unwavering commitment remains.

A calling, a purpose that fuels her soul,
A blueprint for change, a model to extol.
Her work reveals systemic disparities plain,
The need for advocacy, the cry for change.

Resilience and perseverance, lessons learnt,
Confronting battles, no matter how they've churned.
Her career, a testament to relentless drive,
Showing the impact when one strives.

With empathy and voice, change we bring,
Uplifting others, addressing everything.
Her father's plight, a tale of discrimination severe,
Igniting her passion for justice, burning bright and clear.

Transgender rights, bathroom advocacy at hand,
A champion for justice, with a stand so grand.
Her influence on me, values deeply sown,
The fight for justice, now my own.

Justice

Justice, a realisation, made my heart sink. This was something I hadn't done for myself. This was something in a family of strong women and gentle men, they had not encouraged me to do. In my relentless pursuit to uplift others, I had neglected the most important voice of all – my own. I needed to recognise the little girl inside of me who had been silenced for so long.

My five-year-old self, who heard her entire extended family sing "Happy Birthday" only minutes after the first incident of abuse, deserved to be heard.

An innocence had been stolen within the walls of a public toilet, unbeknownst to her family just a short distance away. That little girl couldn't express herself back then. Trauma, confusion, and fear left her mute, unable to convey the grave violation she had suffered.

But now, as an adult, I find the words. Hidden deep, inter-twined with pain and fear, they were there, ready to be unearthed. It's time to inform the police about what this man did to me. Up to now, I had justified my silence by warning other relatives about his behaviour, feeling I couldn't be held responsible if they didn't believe me. I told myself I had done my part, and some days, that felt sufficient.

Until a year ago, I thought it was too late to go to the police, even if I wanted to. But now I knew it was a possibility, the realisation had crept up on me, like the first light of dawn dispelling the darkness of a long, chilly night.

I was seeing evidence everywhere that this was the time to take this next step. It was as if the universe itself had conspired to align the stars, guiding me with signs so unmistakable that I could no longer ignore them.

It felt much the same as when I first recalled the trauma – when memories long buried had surged to the surface, unbidden yet insistent. Back then, a flood of emotions had overwhelmed me. I wasn't ready to remember, to face the raw pain and anguish of those moments. But deep within me, a wiser part of my soul knew I was ready to heal and reclaim the fragments of myself scattered by trauma.

Today, a similar sensation enveloped me. Something else was tapping on my shoulder, both within me and beside me. It was an ethereal presence, a combination of inner strength and external encouragement. Perhaps it was the echoes of supportive voices from my friends, family, or even strangers who unknowingly boosted my resolve. Or maybe it was the persistent whispers of my conscience, urging me towards action, towards justice.

Despite the clamorous symphony of doubt playing in the recesses of my mind, I understood in a profound and intrinsic way that this was my moment. I wasn't ready, but I was. I did not lose sight of the paradox it presented. Feeling prepared or devoid of fear is not always what readiness is about. Despite the physical manifestations of my nervousness, my heart's conviction remained strong, ready to embrace its purpose of pursuing justice and truth.

Not only did I need to do this for myself, but I needed to do it for my children. They are my world, and they must know that it's possible to emerge from traumatic events with strength and grace. They needed to see that confronting and speaking out about our past does not diminish us but fortifies us. My journey could become a blueprint for resilience and empowerment for them, as well as an opportunity for healing for me.

I wanted my five-year-old self to reconnect with the voice taken from her then, 40 years earlier. That stolen voice needed to be reclaimed, not just for me, but for others who might find solace in my story. It's about giving a voice to the silenced parts of us, those hidden chapters that hold immense power and importance.

I had shared my story with my children prior to this day, tailoring it to their age and understanding. I wanted my children to know their voice mattered and I would always hear them if they needed to share anything with me.

I know we can't control all that our children endure, but we can provide a safe place to speak. I can give them that. This was knowledge that in my generation, our parents didn't know they needed to share. I remember my mum saying once after I first recalled my abuse and shared it with her, "I thought it was strangers I needed to keep you safe from".

In the night's silence, I often replay the memories of my childhood, contrasting them against my current state of self-awareness and advocacy. I remind myself of the importance of confronting the darkness within to fully embrace the light.

Returning to the memory of my extended family singing "Happy Birthday" with no knowledge of the trauma I faced moments before, I am filled with a bittersweet realisation. That was a moment stolen from me, a memory tainted by pain. Although I had spoken about my abuse to my family and close friends, I had never gone to the police.

A year before, in 2020, I had a fortuitous conversation with a friend, also a mother, encouraging her children to climb trees during lockdown. We were walking laps around the same oval. She mentioned she had worked in a sexual assault unit early in her law enforcement career.

Our discussion eventually led to my story. "Did you ever report it?" she asked. Naively, I replied, "No, because of the statute of limitations. I thought it was too late by the time I was ready."

"They have lifted that, you know," she shared. "You could go to the police if you ever felt ready."

Almost a year later, I found myself at this march, staring at the word "JUSTICE" as if I were seeing it for the first time. It seemed as if someone had orchestrated the march to bring me to this very moment, to this realisation: it was time.

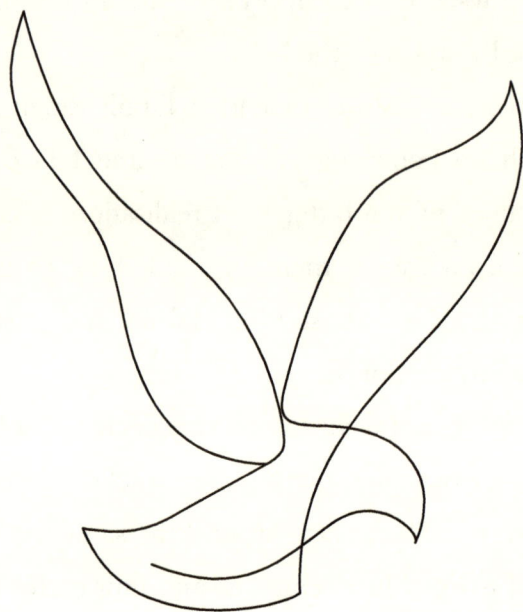

To my five-year-old self that didn't have the words,
That couldn't understand that silent screams won't be heard.
You turned five that day, in the park where you played,
A piece of you lost in the toilet that day.
You were told you were selfish for wanting to leave,
Your nanna made a sponge, we need to sing happy
birthday, act pleased.
He smiled, singing happy birthday with a brown drink
in his hand,
So confused, his actions would take decades to understand.
Until then I shut it away at the back of my mind,
So I could be happy and smile and continue to be kind.
So I could go back to kindergarten and play mums and dads,
And work hard to keep my babies safe from anyone that
might be bad.

Chapter Three

Police

After attending the protest, I took my kids to school as usual, but my mind was in turmoil. Instead of going home, I found myself driving aimlessly through town. The sight of open shops after so many Covid shutdowns was a welcome surprise. I decided to stop at a local boutique to buy a skirt for a work function.

When the saleswoman asked me about what was on for the rest of my day, I blurted out without thinking, "I am going to police to report a sexual assault." I briefly second-guessed whether I had spoken aloud, but her stunned silence confirmed I had.

My admission seemed to solidify the situation, emphasising the gravity of my next steps. After leaving the store, I got into my car, driven by a force beyond my own conscious understanding, compelling me to act. It was real now; I had voiced it out loud. It had to be done.

Sitting in my car just outside the local police station, I grappled with doubt about whether this was the correct initial step. If I was honest with myself, beyond the previous understanding that I only had two years after remembering to report the abuse, I just hadn't been ready to do this before that day.

It had required years of therapy to reach a point where I could even contemplate any legal avenue. Now, 23 years past my memories surfacing, and there I sat at the threshold of the station, torn between remaining encased in the car's familiar confines or mustering the courage to step through those glass doors into uncertainty. Indecision and resolve churned within me. I hadn't told anyone but the woman in the store my plans.

The entire day felt predestined – the march, the word on the sand, looking at my children and their innocent faces, reminding me of my own innocence when the incidents occurred in my childhood.

I felt a presence with me, whether it was an angel or a spirit guide, I wasn't sure. It felt as though I was out of my body, and something else was moving me. I felt the support of my legs – one foot, then the next. I felt like I was being held, metaphorically and physically. So much of me wasn't ready for this, but so much of me was.

I felt the strength of the women in my life, both living and those who had passed, including my grandmothers. Their strength enveloped me, and I had never felt so guided towards something in my entire life. I entered the police station. The room was eerily quiet, completely unlike the bustling scenes you see in the movies.

No one was at the front desk. I approached the desk, and a police officer emerged from behind the glass. Perhaps he anticipated a minor complaint, like a lost item or a minor traffic incident. Contrary to such expectations, the words that left my mouth were firm and unexpected: "I would like to report a sexual assault."

The officer's face registered a flicker of surprise before he quickly composed himself. He asked, "When did this incident occur?"

I took a deep breath and replied, "1981." His eyebrows lifted, and for a moment, the gravity of my words seemed to hang between us. He nodded slowly and motioned for me to follow him into a quieter, more private room.

It was a small room with plain walls and a simple table with a few chairs. The starkness of the room felt almost comforting, as if it had been stripped down to focus on the gravity of the conversations held within its walls. As I sat down, the officer offered me tea and began to ask me more detailed questions.

Each query pulled at memories I had tried to keep buried for decades, but now was the time to unearth them. As I recounted my story, I felt a strange mixture of vulnerability and empowerment. This moment was something I had feared for so long, yet I also felt a sense of liberation in finally giving voice to my past.

The officer listened attentively, jotting down notes and occasionally nodding in understanding. He did not rush me, giving me time to collect my thoughts and emotions. I appreciated his patience and the dignity he afforded me. It made this daunting process slightly more bearable.

Finally, after what felt like an eternity, he leaned back in his chair and said, "Thank you for sharing this with me. I understand how difficult this must have been for you. Firstly, we need to confirm if the abuser is still alive. I'll look into this today and let you know."

With trembling soul, I walk towards the station door,
A story etched in silence, now ready to soar.
Bracing myself for the words I must say,
To share my truth, to light the way.

The weight of silence, a burden I bear,
Deep within, the memories tear.
But in this moment of courage, I find my voice,
To speak the unspeakable, to make a choice.

Through quivering lips, the words find release,
Each syllable a step towards peace.
The room envelops me, a mix of fear and relief,
As I share the tale of my pain and grief.

The officer listens, their gaze intent,
Offering support, a safe ascent.
No judgement, no doubt, just a space to confide,
In their hands, my truth does reside.

With each detail shared, a piece of me heals,
The darkness recedes, my spirit reveals.
Courage blooms in the face of the night,
As I stand in the police station's light.

To break the silence, to speak my truth,
To face the shadows of my youth.
In this moment of courage, I find my strength,
To reclaim my voice, regardless of length.

And as I leave, a weight lifted off my chest,
A journey begun; a truth confessed.
With newfound resolve, I walk away,
Knowing that in speaking out, I am on my way.

Alive

Alive. The word hit me with unexpected force. It hadn't occurred to me that he could be dead. My mind raced – please don't be dead. I need this. I need to tell my story and feel the weight lift.

I need you to know that you didn't beat me. I am strong and happy, and I have built a good life despite your attempts to destroy it. I didn't realise how much I needed this until now, until the possibility arises that I may not be able to do it at all.

As a child, I wished you gone, out of sight,
To avoid the pain, to escape the fight.
But now, I want you alive, in my stare,
So, justice falls, standing fair and square.

The wronged little girl now a woman of worth,
No longer defined by your shadow's girth.
In me, you see the victory you failed to claim,
For I am the phoenix rising from your shame.

Covid

The call came from the original police officer I had encountered earlier that day: "We have confirmation that this man is alive."

A mixture of relief and trepidation flooded me in that moment. He showed kindness and would be one of seven law enforcement officers who would support me on this difficult journey. He was one of only two I would have the opportunity to meet face to face.

As the year was 2021, amid the Covid-19 pandemic, Victoria was experiencing a series of sudden lockdowns.

With each cycle, we would hear from Premier Dan Andrews, urging us into isolation for our collective wellbeing. In my heart, I hoped that these measures were truly in everyone's best interest, so we obliged. During this period, it was my goal to shield my children from the chaos, minimise the disruption to their lives and to make this time meaningful for us.

In every challenge I've faced, I've found purpose. Transitioning to new schools in both primary and high school, I viewed it as a chance to expand my circle of friends. Following two consecutive losses at school swimming sports, I committed to rigorous training every morning at 5 am until I triumphed over one competitor. After enduring a pregnancy loss, I channelled my sorrow into writing, infusing that painful chapter with significance and birthing a book into the world instead.

During the pandemic, I was determined to make this period valuable for me and my family.

I asked myself, *How can I make this time count?*

The inability to contribute outwardly to family and friends turned into an odd form of freedom for me. I couldn't look after anyone else, so there was space to focus on my own family, which required me to really look closely at my own place within it.

I recognised that Covid brought complexity and varied realities for everyone, each person navigating the storm in their own way. I also understand that our experience was less severe than many. We were in a fortunate position: although my consulting work had decreased and my pride took a hit, my husband's business was thriving with activity.

Residing in regional Victoria proved to be advantageous, with milder lockdown restrictions and nature at our doorstep – beaches for swimming and surfing, and ample trees for climbing.

My attention turned to educating our young son in kindergarten and our grade three daughter at home. After initially resisting the change, I eventually found joy in this new routine; we would complete the day's lessons by 9 am, allowing us time for lengthy walks, homemade pasta sessions, and constructing forts.

Of course, the journey wasn't without its challenges. There were evenings when I'd retreat to a soothing bath with a glass of wine by 4:30 pm, signalling a particularly trying day to my husband.

In my focus to make this time meaningful, I envisioned a future where I'd look back with gratitude, knowing that I utilised this period to our advantage rather than letting it defeat us. As

I played the most significant role in influencing my children during this time, with no friends and no teachers or other family members, I asked myself, *What do I want to be responsible for teaching them?*

I decided that I wanted to impart the value of enduring boredom, entertaining themselves without technology, cooking, knitting, making their own beds, writing letters, riding bikes, bush walking, playing cards, drawing, and a fundamental life skill of tackling the tasks you need to do first so you can enjoy the activities you want to do afterward.

Fundamentally, I wanted to teach and model to my children how to manage strong emotions. They were learning that sometimes life is out of our control, and so, what better time to approach this next step for me, delving into the investigation of my childhood sexual assault.

A storm of worries plagued my thoughts:

What if the police don't believe my story?

Will my loved ones dismiss this pursuit as futile?

How will this impact my kids?

Might this endeavour plunge me into darkness, a place from which I couldn't emerge?

Despite these fears gripping me, I recognised the necessity of this next phase as it was all that was left to do in my healing.

The complexity of Covid is hard to ignore,
But I used this time to settle the score,
To go to the police for the wrongs you did to me,
My strength and resilience for my children to see.

I used that time to become whole,
To heal my heart and fuel my soul,
Twenty-three years later, the truth in my hand,
Seeking justice, taking a stand.

In the midst of a pandemic's strain,
I found the courage to break the chain,
No longer silent, no longer subdued,
Speaking out, healing the wounds imbued.

The isolation brought introspection, a chance to grow,
To confront the past, to let the truth flow,

For my children to witness my fight,
For them to see the power of standing in the light,
Using this time as a catalyst for change,
In the midst of chaos, finding my range.

Witness Statement

The next step was to meet with a detective in a dedicated department for sexual assault. Once I arrived at the police station, the detective's firm but compassionate demeanour offered comfort, affirming that coming forward was significant, that my story had worth. This was a significant moment in the investigation; this conversation with the detective in the sexual assault department was a two-hour meeting.

The story was told to this detective, in more detail, with more depth.

He stated, "It is evident to me that a crime has indeed occurred." He added, "Kath, I believe you. Before you proceed, I must share some facts with you. It's estimated that only 23 per cent of sexual assault victims report the crime. From those cases, less than 10 per cent of childhood sexual assault cases lead to a trial, and of those, only one per cent result in a conviction."

My immediate thought was, *Is this worth it? Should I really put myself through this?*

Then, I felt the presence of my confused eight-year-old self, a little girl who couldn't understand why she had been abused again. It was for her that I decided to move forward.

In that moment of revelation, a heavy truth descends,
Only 23 per cent come forth, the silence never ends.
Such a small fraction seeks justice's door,
And even fewer see the trial floor.

A mere 10 per cent make it to the legal stage,
Where stories unfold, page by page.
But the path to conviction, oh so slim,
Only one per cent find justice's hymn.

These numbers speak volumes of a system amiss,
Of voices unheard, of pain dismissed.
The conversation must shift, the narrative reframed,
To empower the silenced, ignite the flame.

Statistics revealed, anger stirs within,
This goes beyond me, beneath all our skin.
My abuser not alone in bearing this shame,
One of many, we aim to reframe.
A complex conversation long overdue,
So, abuser, this is no longer just about just me and you.

Shifting the Focus

During this time, I continued to focus on making each day count. I poured my energy into homeschooling, ensuring my kids felt supported and loved despite the upheaval. I embraced the slower pace as an opportunity to reconnect with my inner child, asking what she wanted to do today – a question I had not had the luxury of asking for a very long time.

Every creative outlet I embraced became a lifeline, a way to channel my turbulent emotions into something tangible and meaningful. Writing became my ally, allowing me to express with words what needed to be said, with my children sitting alongside, unlike talking on a phone where inevitably one of them would follow me to listen out of curiosity.

As the investigation stretched on, the lockdowns became a part of our new normal. It was a complex, turbulent time. What would the outcome be? How long would it go on? Would life ever go back to normal again? High emotions surfaced for many, and we were all struggling in our own way, so I didn't really have much opportunity for support from friends or family.

In the quiet moments, when fear tried to creep back in, I reminded myself of why I was doing this. This was about reclaiming my narrative, asserting my strength, and setting an example for my children that courage and resilience can triumph over trauma. I cherished the time with my kids. It brought us closer, and I learnt more about how they think, what motivates them, and what drives their curiosity. In many ways, it was a gift. But there was no escaping the ongoing investigation. The reality of it was ever-present, with little room for distraction.

During that period, my husband was my primary support, as everyone else was dealing with their own challenges. We met friends at the football oval occasionally, sipping wine from coffee cups while the kids played; as the parks were closed, this became their playground.

My daughter struggled with the isolation; she missed her friends, school, and activities like netball and dance. So, I made sure she stayed connected to as many people as possible within the restrictions. In contrast, my son thrived during lockdown. With unrestricted access to me, the ocean, his bike, and hours exploring the nearby bushland, he was content.

The four of us formed a tight-knit team, and I explained the situation to my kids in a G-rated version regarding the investigation and my abuse.

When I first came home from the Geelong police station, my son asked me if "he was in jail yet?" My son's innocent words of encouragement struck a chord deep within me. It made me ponder the weight of seeking justice – did I truly want this man to be behind bars?

What would others think of me for pursuing this path of holding him accountable for his actions? Were my son's questions a reflection of the justice and righteousness that needed to prevail in this situation? Or was seeking retribution going too far, especially when I was aware that others had endured far more severe injustices than I had? Contemplating the dictionary definition of justice, with its emphasis on righteousness, equitableness, and moral rightness, made me reconsider my acceptance of my abuse.

Why did I stay silent for so long?
Why did it take me a lifetime to undo your wrong?

Twenty-three years after, I remember my abuse,
I walk into a police station, seeking justice, searching
for truth.

The weight of shame, the burden of guilt,
Kept me hidden, my pain deeply built,

But with each passing day, the truth grew strong,
And the courage within finally felt like it belonged.

Conditioned

Had I believed that it was just my place to put up with the bad behaviour of men around me? Was it simply my job to avoid as much of it as possible and push away the bad memories so that I could go on living a happy life?

The definition of justice is the administration of law, and the determination of rights based on principles of fairness and reason; it calls for action.

Recalling the story of my friend's younger sister who suffered at the hands of a gymnastic coach, I couldn't help but empathise with the pain and trauma that the young girls endured. The coach's appalling actions of violating their bodies and invading their privacy left me questioning the depths of my own past experiences of abuse.

Reflecting on my initial reaction, "Was that all he did, and he went to jail?" I realised I had become desensitised to mistreatment and normalised the unacceptable behaviours that I had faced throughout my life. In this private response, I felt ashamed.

Were all those instances of abuse, harassment, and exploitation a reflection of a distorted perception of what was deemed tolerable? Like most women, I have had many moments to desensitise me.

I recall a time when I was walking from school to a sleepover in grade six with a group of friends, a man who was running pulled at his running shorts as he approached us, and his penis came out as he ran by.

This incident gave us hours of gossip, and I think we all silently felt impacted and disturbed by this, but we didn't know it was a crime. Maybe we thought it was an accident? Did we even think to tell an adult about this? I can't remember.

Then there was the man at high school who was masturbating under his jacket while sitting opposite me on the train. I got off a stop early. Did I tell my mum about this, or was I too embarrassed?

When I shared it with friends at school, many of them, too, had similar stories to share.

Then there was the time we were warned about a man exposing himself to young girls at Caulfield station. This warning came from the school after several of us experienced an incident of exposure. We were already learning it was our responsibility to be in pairs, not to go to the toilet alone at the station, and to rearrange our plans to keep ourselves safe. It was up to us, and we accepted this without question instead of asking for a change in how we experienced our simple commute to school.

Had the abuse I suffered as a child become normalised in my mind, serving as a benchmark for what I considered acceptable behaviour from men? It seemed that I had grown accustomed to overlooking the mistreatment and disrespect from men, as if it was just a part of life.

I wasn't alone in this experience – many women that I knew had their own stories of facing mistreatment, whether it was minor incidents or life-altering events. We were all too familiar with being subjected to inappropriate behaviour, derogatory remarks, and discriminatory treatment.

It made me wonder if my past trauma had conditioned me to prioritise my own safety above all else, to the point where I would tolerate mistreatment to avoid conflict or further harm.

Perhaps I had subconsciously internalised the belief that it was my responsibility to protect myself from harm, rather than holding others accountable for their actions.

As a result, I found myself constantly on guard, always alert for signs of potential danger and trying to avoid attracting negative attention in the first place. My childhood abuse had shaped me into a survivor, but at what cost?

I recall a dinner outing with my stepfather and my brother, who had a friend over for the evening. They were engaged in some light-hearted banter when my brother suggested sharing a joke the scout leader had told them.

His friend initially hesitated, noting that they had been advised not to share it. Despite the warning, the joke was shared, revealing disturbing undertones of this man and what I now understand as early grooming.

The joke opened an opportunity to share that I had experienced discomfort with the same scout leader when a hug in the kitchen had left me feeling extremely uncomfortable. I disclosed this incident to my family, leading to our decision not to return to the scout group. In retrospect, I minimised the significance of the incident, comparing it to the abuse I had endured from my abuser. I considered myself fortunate that the situation hadn't escalated further, dismissing it as a mere brush with discomfort.

As a mother now and after years of witnessing these incidents for myself and others, the fierce protection and love I felt for my children only intensified my resolve to step up and talk about these acts. The mere thought of anyone harming my children filled me with a righteous anger and a determination to see perpetrators face the consequences of their actions.

The realisation that the abuser had committed violent acts against me as an innocent child reignited a raging fire within me. His despicable behaviour had caused irreparable harm and inflicted wounds that no child should ever have to endure.

It had set me up for an unfair understanding of how to set boundaries and what to expect from the adults in my life. I was lucky to have good adults around me; not everyone who experienced abuse early does. It is no wonder that they enter relationships that are unhealthy or abusive; that is all some people ever know.

It compelled me to confront the harsh reality of the injustices that plague our society and reinforced the importance of standing up for oneself and others in the pursuit of truth and justice. One in three girls and one in six boys are abused worldwide before the age of 18.[2] We must change this conversation; we must start to do better.

We must all contribute to this change if we want a different experience for our children. It must start now, and I have to do my part. Any act, small or large, needed to have consequences.

Everything is triggering the lost little girl inside me,

She is wrapped up in a ball as tight as can be.

Staying vigilant to the danger that might come her way,

Alert to what surrounds her all night and all day.

A healing to remind me what is supporting me now.

The presence of an angel guiding this little girl to how.

How to shine and to soar above all this pain,

How to connect and to love and be happy again.

Staying connected to you will lead me to my inner light,

Staying connected to you will support me to continue this fight.

I trust in the process; trust life is happening for me,

I trust in me in becoming who I am meant to be.

Remembering

As a child, I was a bright and spirited girl known for her sense of humour, athleticism, and creativity. I was surrounded by strong women who confidently spoke their truth and stood up for what's right.

My cheerful and outgoing nature made me well-liked among my peers, and my athletic prowess earned me respect on the netball court and in the pool. To everyone else, I imagine I seemed happy, easy-going and the kind of girl who could handle anything life threw her way.

At times, I wonder why it took me so long to go to the police about what happened to me, why I remained silent. In reflection, the reasons for my memories staying locked up are complex.

I was living in Darwin after finishing uni, a challenging experience with homesickness and bouts of depression weighing heavily on my mind. During this difficult period, my close-knit group of friends from school became my anchor, offering unwavering support as we navigated our individual paths and life changes together.

The excitement of two close friends getting married within a week of each other prompted me to save up and plan a trip back home to attend both celebrations. It was in the lead-up to this visit that my mum, recognising the decline in my mental health, arranged for me to see a psychologist to address my struggles when I was home in Melbourne.

I arrived at Melbourne airport and got picked up by girls I went to school with and who had been in my world for years. We navigated all the breakups, stress of study, and friendship bumps and bruises that anyone lucky enough to have real, close female friends get to live through.

The first wedding was that night and so fun, so much laughter and dancing; this was the first of our group to get married, so we had a ball!

Monday morning was my first session with the psychologist. The therapist's kind demeanour created a safe space for me to open up, leading to a pivotal moment as I was leaving the session where I said, "I am scared of older men, is that normal?"

This admission marked the first step towards unravelling the tightly held memories that had haunted me for so long.

As I delved deeper into therapy the next day, the floodgates of suppressed memories began to open, overwhelming me with flashes of a past filled with darkness, fear, and confusion.

Nothing was surfacing but I could feel the fear; my body remembered before my mind did.

My abuser was a heavy drinker, and his drink of choice was brown, so the therapist brought whiskey into the third session. He got me to smell the drink and through other support in that third session, the flood gates opened. The intense emotional upheaval triggered physical manifestations, leaving me feeling like I was spiralling out of control, desperately seeking a way to stop the torrent of memories.

Returning to my mum's place after the session, the relentless twitches and tremors persisted, prompting me to seek immediate help and return to the psychologist that afternoon. The subsequent sessions unravelled a cascade of memories, each one a piece of a painful puzzle that had shaped my perception of myself and the world around me.

Questions swarmed around me like sharks:

Why didn't I tell anyone at the time?

Why didn't I speak up then?

How did I let it happen again?

Why didn't anyone know?

Why didn't someone stop him?

Is it my fault?

Is it their fault?

Is it his fault?

Flashes of images flicker: cake, darkness, eyes shut, floating, choking, ducks, singing, they are singing to me, tree, happy birthday, slide, crying, toilet, cake, nausea, smiling, why are they smiling, am I smiling, I want to go home now. Why can't they see I want to go home now?

My body shakes and twitches uncontrollably. *What's happening?*

Feelings long locked away are surging out, trying to spill everywhere all at once.

I can't stop it; I don't understand it. *Where has this been hiding all this time?*

How has it been inside me, locked away in my mind?

Depression went from being an unwanted friend you hoped you didn't get seated next to at a dinner party to a crazy stalker that I couldn't escape. Depression was a gentle knocking from pandoras box until this therapist finally held my hand while I opened it.

The box was open now, and I desperately wanted to shove the lid back on, but there was too much spilling out. It wouldn't all fit back in. The box was open, the pieces were everywhere and now I had to figure out where to place all these pieces and make sense of them once and for all.

That day of remembering, I revealed my painful truth to those closest to me; it was hard to say the word 'abused'; there was no way I was ready to call the act anything else. I was still coming to terms with it, like I was watching someone else go through this. Someone else that wasn't me. I felt like I was out of my body, without any knowledge of how I was going to get back in, or even if it was safe to do so.

The journey of healing had only just begun, and remembering felt like a whole new trauma I would have to navigate on its own.

Speaking out marked a crucial step towards reclaiming my voice and narrative, but it didn't make me feel any less alone.

Instead, it made me feel more isolated and confused.

I thought I had a good childhood.

I thought I was happy.

I thought I was lucky.

I thought I knew myself.

I thought I was strong.

How could I have let this happen?

How could I have forgotten about it?

So much self-loathing followed the remembering; this felt like I was being retraumatised all over again, at 23 years old.

The day I spoke the truth aloud,
To friends, my story I avowed.
Abuse, a word with heavy weight,
Unveiling memories, sealing fate.

My body, a vessel of whispered pain,
Twitching, trembling, a battle gained.
As past and present intertwined,
In echoes of trauma, a soul confined.

Dissociating

I questioned everything I once believed to be true.

How can I trust what I see?

How can I trust what I always thought was real?

How can I trust anyone, especially myself?

But at least I had spoken out and shared my truth. Apparently, that makes me brave, as I've been told not everyone dares to do this. Sometimes I think it would have been brave to not tell anyone, to not subject my family and friends to such pain. But without sharing this about my life I would not have survived; I know it would have swallowed me whole and I would die without anyone knowing my truth. I believe this happens more than we will ever know.

This was why I had no choice; I wouldn't have survived much longer without knowing. My body no longer was able to carry the weight and my mind no longer able to suppress the pain.

Now the new challenge: I must see if I can survive the knowing. At this point, I wasn't sure which was worse.

When a child experiences sexual assault, it profoundly affects their brain and emotional development. Imagine that a child's brain is like a young tree still growing its branches and roots. Trauma acts like a violent storm, striking this delicate tree and impacting its growth in various ways.

Firstly, there's the hippocampus, crucial for forming and retrieving memories. During and after severe stress or trauma, the hippocampus doesn't develop properly and doesn't function well. This impairment makes it difficult for the child to create detailed, coherent memories of the traumatic event.

Then there's the amygdala, which processes emotions, especially fear. In the case of childhood sexual assault, the child's amygdala can become hyperactive. This heightened sensitivity makes the emotional content of memories overwhelming. To cope, the brain often suppresses these memories to protect the child from being consumed by fear and distress.

The prefrontal cortex, responsible for decision-making and impulse control, also gets affected. Trauma can disrupt its normal functions, altering how memories are processed and stored. When these brain regions are under such stress, the child may not form clear memories at all, or they might store the memories in fragmented bits that are hard to piece together later.

Children often respond to trauma by dissociating. This means they might mentally distance themselves from the event, almost like watching it happen to someone else or feeling like they're outside their own body.

My memories are from the roof; I floated up above the incident and watched it from outside of my body. I believe this was what allowed me to maintain a happy childhood.

Dissociation can result in fragmented or incomplete memories, it is the case for me; some things are stored in my body, some stored as feelings, some as thoughts. I was five years old when the first incident of abuse happened. I had no understanding of violence, least of all sexual violence. I knew what was done to me hurt, I was scared, there was shame, but I didn't have the language to speak about it. My body didn't have the maturity to process it, and the innocent little girl who had her whole family at the park for her birthday didn't want to seem ungrateful and spoil the party. As I resurfaced from the bathroom, nothing had changed for anyone else at the park that day, although for me, nothing would ever be the same.

Children cope by repressing memories, a protective mechanism of the brain to shield the child from unbearable psychological pain. The brain hides these traumatic memories away in a mental 'vault'.

Children might also practice cognitive avoidance. They actively distract themselves and avoid thinking about the abuse, often engaging in various activities to keep their minds occupied. Over time, this avoidance becomes a habitual coping strategy, increasing the likelihood that traumatic memories will stay suppressed.

Moreover, the stress responses activated during trauma, like the release of cortisol, add another layer of complexity. Cortisol, a stress hormone, can impair the brain regions responsible for memory and emotional regulation. It's like a constant surge of stress that makes it hard to store clear, coherent memories.

The body's immediate response to trauma, often referred to as the 'fight or flight' response, directs resources away from memory formation towards immediate survival.

The brain prioritises survival over memory storage, resulting in incomplete or jumbled memories, particularly when you also add the complexity of the abuser being known to the victim like in 94 per cent of cases, or like in my case related to the victim, which is also common in 50 per cent of childhood sexual assault cases.[3]

It's a complex interplay of brain chemistry, emotional shielding, and external influences that can keep traumatic memories locked away, only to resurface later when the individual is perhaps more equipped to deal with them, or when some external circumstance triggers their return. In adults, this often happens when becoming parents themselves.

Body shattered, mind fractured, left behind,
Adrift in confusion, hurts entwined.
As chaos reigns, my spirit takes flight,
In search of solace, craving the light.

Who's left to bear the burdens of trauma's weight,
Who carries the pain, locked in a sealed fate?
When all parts scatter, who's there to recall,
Can lost fragments return, after the fall?

From scattered whispers, untold truths arise,
Piecing together what the darkness belies.
Drawing shards close, forging connections anew,
In fragmented pasts, seeking wholeness true.

In a mirror of shards, a reflection of broken parts,
Dissociation scatters, unearthing hidden hearts.
Was it my flesh that lingered in the pain's domain,
While my liberated mind sought to regain?

Where did my spirit wander off and steer,
Through life's tumultuous journey, ever clear?
Gathering the enigma, sowing seeds unknown,
In unity, striving to reclaim each part shown.

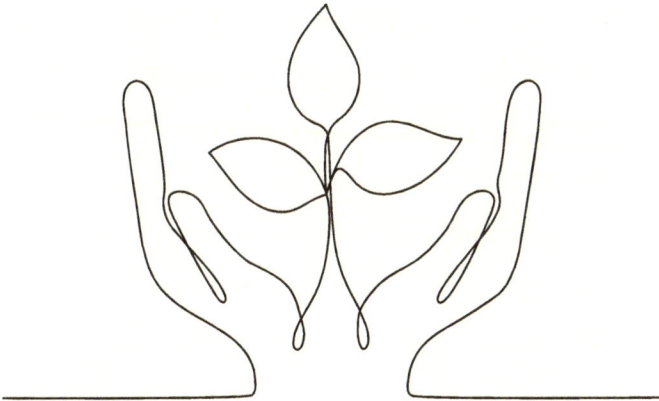

23 Years

It took me over 23 years to finally come to terms with what had happened and to report it to the police. I did make sure that it was known to the family what this person had done. I was concerned about other children in the family being hurt.

Many who know me would describe me as incredibly strong and capable, yet I spent decades processing the abuse, feeling shame, guilt, anger, sadness, confusion, frustration, and pain. For 23 years, the police had no knowledge of my abuse.

It is easy to say: I wish I had done it sooner. But the truth was, it is never easy to relive trauma, no matter how ready you are to face it.

Studies have shown that survivors often face personal disbelief and external doubt when they come forward about abuse by someone they know, unlike when they report abuse by a stranger.[4] This can be incredibly discouraging and may prevent survivors from receiving the support and validation they need.

This must change. The statistics speak for themselves.

To bring about change and prevent future abuse, it is necessary to acknowledge and address the real issue. It will require a shift in societal attitudes and beliefs, as well as providing survivors with the help and support they need. It is time to break the cycle of abuse and create a safer and more supportive environment for survivors to be heard when they do speak out.

Coming forward as a survivor of abuse is a difficult and courageous act. It requires a tremendous amount of strength and vulnerability to share one's story.

However, keeping the experience to yourself can be even more detrimental. The weight of the trauma can become unbearable when carried alone. It is necessary to acknowledge and address the issue, not only for oneself but also to break the cycle of abuse and create a safer environment for future generations.

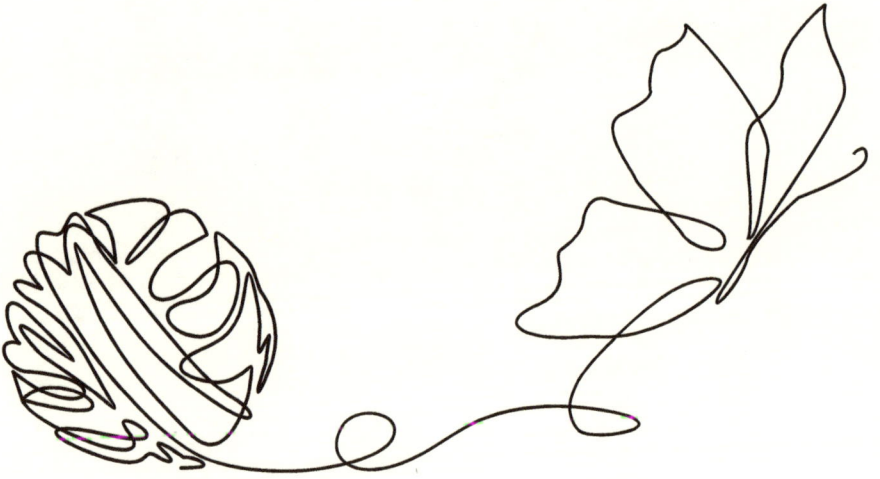

As a child bearing the unseen weight,
The first challenge, a burden to abate.
Memories flooding back, the second test,
Reclaiming truths, a journey to invest.

Integration of identity, a path to retrace,
Weaving threads of self in healing's grace.
Then triggers of motherhood, emotions unfurled,
A new perspective on the pain of the world.

The burden of truth to heal for them,
Creating change to guide their stem.
But realisation dawns, a truth anew,
That I, too, deserved healing's rescue.

Last, my inner child, a presence near,
Innocence waiting, feelings sincere.
Nurturing her journey, with love to mend,
Embracing the past, as we build and ascend.

Listen

This shift in societal attitudes and beliefs is crucial in creating a supportive environment for survivors. Society often blames and shames the victim, adding to their burden and making it harder for them to come forward. It takes immense courage to speak up and seek help, but it takes even more to believe and support a survivor. Those who have the capacity to listen and believe are invaluable allies in the healing journey. They create a space of safety and comfort, enabling the survivor to share their truth and begin the process of healing. Providing survivors with the help and support they need is essential in their healing journey.

This support could range from therapy and counselling to a supportive network of friends and family. No two experiences are the same, and therefore, each survivor's needs are unique. It is crucial to create a safe and supportive environment for survivors, as it allows them to break free from the trauma and move towards a healthier and happier life. It is time to break the cycle of abuse and create a better world for survivors.

By actively listening and acknowledging their stories, we can show survivors that their voices matter and that they are not alone. Reflecting on our own experiences and reaching critical self-awareness can greatly influence our life narrative. It allows us to connect the dots between our past choices and the person we have become. By acknowledging and understanding our past traumas and experiences, we can make more informed and intentional decisions in our present and future.

This can lead to personal growth and the creation of a more positive and fulfilling life story. It is important to continuously reflect and learn from our experiences, as they shape who we are and the choices we make.

In shifting attitudes, beliefs take hold,
Creating a space, supportive and bold.
Blame and shame, burdens to untie,
For survivors to soar, to reach the sky.
Courage to speak, to seek the light,
Belief and support, a beacon bright.
In allies who listen, in those who believe,
Survivors find solace, a chance to retrieve.

Resurfacing

After I remembered the first incident, more memories of my childhood trauma began to resurface. The experience was incredibly complex and emotionally charged. At first, I didn't even recognise what was happening. It was like a fog had lifted, and suddenly I was confronted with a flood of emotions and images I had long buried deep within my mind. The initial wave of emotions was the hardest to bear. The fear and anxiety were so intense that I felt like I was reliving the trauma all over again. There were days when I couldn't distinguish between the past and the present. The fear that had gripped me during those harrowing experiences as a child returned with a vengeance, as if the years between then and now had evaporated.

Every shadow and every sudden noise would make my heart race uncontrollably. Alongside the fear, I was overwhelmed by a profound sense of sadness and grief. I mourned the lost innocence of my childhood and grieved for the person I might have become had the trauma never occurred. It was as though I was feeling the weight of a lost future, filled with opportunities and dreams that were stolen from me.

Then there was the anger – white-hot rage that consumed me. I was furious at my abuser and enraged at the people who should have protected me but didn't. How did no one notice?

This rage often turned inward, morphing into a suffocating sense of self-blame and shame. I found myself trapped in a vicious cycle of anger and guilt, questioning my worth and battling destructive thoughts.

The confusion and disorientation were equally unsettling. There were moments when I doubted the authenticity of my memories. Had those horrible things really happened, or was my mind playing tricks on me?

The dissonance between what I had always believed and what I was now remembering left me questioning my sanity. It was a dizzying experience, trying to reconcile these resurfacing memories with the life I thought I knew.

My body reacted as vividly and violently as my mind. Sometimes, memories would trigger a physical response – sweating, heart palpitations, nausea, and even pain in parts of my body connected to the abuse. These reactions were distressingly real, making the whole experience feel even more tangible and immediate.

Panic attacks plagued me, and there were times I felt as though jumping out of the moving car would be less painful than simply sitting still in the seat where all my internal organs felt like they were trying to jump out of me all at once. These panic attacks would strike out of nowhere, a freight train of dread hurtling through me. My breath would become short, ragged gasps, my heart pounding like a drum in my chest.

Dizzy spells would follow, where the world tilted and spun, and I'd be overwhelmed by a crushing sense of impending doom. These episodes were debilitating, adding another layer of terror to an already overwhelming experience.

Flashbacks were some of the worst moments. They were intense, vivid episodes where I felt like I was back in those haunting moments, living them all over again.

The sensory details – the sights, sounds, and even smells – were so precise that I couldn't tell them apart from reality. It was as if time had folded in on itself, and the boundaries between past and present ceased to exist. These flashbacks were utterly consuming, leaving me feeling drained and alone.

My perception of the world around me shifted dramatically as well. I started to reevaluate my entire past, piecing together behaviours and feelings that had previously made little sense. It was like seeing my life through a new, albeit painful, lens. I noticed gaps in my memory and discrepancies between what I had known and what I was now recalling. This disorientation left me feeling like a stranger in my own life.

Behaviourally, I found myself developing avoidance mechanisms. I would steer clear of certain places or people that triggered memories, even if it meant isolating myself from social circles and familiar environments. To this day, I will avoid entering a public toilet on my own.

Simple things like a song or a scent could send me spiralling, so I built invisible walls around myself, trying to create a haven, albeit a lonely one. Amidst all this chaos, I fought to find a semblance of peace.

Therapy became a lifeline, a place where I could untangle the knot of memories and emotions. While the process was slow and fraught with setbacks, it offered a glimmer of hope. Slowly, I learnt coping mechanisms, grounded myself in the present, and began to navigate the labyrinth of my past without being consumed by it.

This journey of resurfacing memories is ongoing, filled with peaks and valleys. Facing these memories head-on, as painful as it is, opens the door to healing. And while the shadows of the past may never fully disappear, confronting them has revealed strength I never knew I possessed.

I was fortunate to have support around me during those dark days. There were moments I am embarrassed about, like picking up a rock in a fit of rage and throwing it through my housemate's car window after a heated discussion – my misplaced anger being channelled into the moment. The pain ran deep within me, taking over all the parts of my identity that I related to the most. I was lost and had no idea who I was becoming.

My friends from home were a constant support and reminder of the impermanence of this current state. One friend joked with me that throwing that rock and paying for the replacement window was cheaper and more effective than hours of therapy.

Anger was not a comfortable emotion for me to express. The morning after this incident occurred, I knew I had gone too far; evidence that I needed help. I needed to get home to Melbourne to my friends and family, where the support network I needed was all there.

I snuck out the next morning and called a cab; the cab driver thought I was fleeing from a domestic situation where I wasn't safe. I had to tell him it was me who wasn't to be trusted, that I think I was going crazy and needed help. "Please take me to the hospital to get help," I begged.

He turned the meter off and sat with me outside the mental hospital. He said that he didn't think that was where I needed to be. He suggested that I walk inside and get a feel for what my gut said once I walked in. He offered to wait outside and would happily drive me anywhere else if it didn't feel right. I walked through the doors and started down the stale white corridors; hospitals all smell the same.

They mostly look the same, but the feeling I had within those walls was new – pain, sadness, and my gut told me to get the hell out of there as fast as I could. That cab driver was like a guardian angel, who had spent time in that hospital, he would tell me after I returned. He wished he hadn't. He drove me to a hotel where I proceeded to sleep for 24 hours.

I wasn't losing my mind; I was grappling with grief, depression, and PTSD. I was far from my family, struggling to find my identity. I owe my life to that compassionate man who guided me towards seeking the help I desperately needed that day.

I often pondered the timing of those memories resurfacing – was it because I was far from home, or did it coincide with my grandfather's passing?

It wasn't until recently that I made the connection to my brother's 21st birthday party when everything changed. Dressed in a wild wig and '70s-themed attire, surrounded by loved ones at the celebration, I felt a sense of joy.

But then, I saw him, my abuser, whom I hadn't encountered in years. His presence sparked discomfort within me; his obliviousness to my existence struck a deep chord. The lack of recognition ignited surprising anger within me. Unable to shake off the unsettling emotions of this encounter, I tried to attribute my depression to my move to Darwin.

However, the intensity of my feelings refused to be ignored. That night, as I lay in bed, I delved into why his presence made me so uneasy and why, as a child, I always avoided being near him. I realised that I had never felt that way with anyone else in my life. It left me wondering why.

The pain of trauma echoes deep within,
But the agony of remembering begins.
A door to a realm untold,
A new path to navigate, a story to unfold.
How do I bear this pain in my core,
Without losing myself in the shadows once more?
How do I stand firm in the face of despair,
When my body's enveloped in fear's cold snare?
Making sense of the impossible, a daunting task,
Yet my body speaks truths I cannot mask.
Guided by inner whispers, a compass unseen,
Nudging me towards light, through scenes unclean.
I strive to hold onto hope, to grasp the faintest thread,
Amidst the turmoil, the chaos widespread.
In the midst of darkness, seeking a glimmer, a spark,
Navigating the shadows, into the new I embark.

Chapter Four

Pieces of the Puzzle

During the investigation, the case was to be transferred to the jurisdiction where the incidents had occurred. This meant that the new investigating police department would take over the case, not the officer who had initially taken my statement and sat with me for two hours.

Instead, a woman in Melbourne would be handling it. Due to the complexities of Covid-19, it was decided that the witness statement would be taken in Geelong, where travel restrictions were less stringent compared to Melbourne.

The time was set for me to provide my full witness statement, and the detective warned me that it would be an emotional and gruelling process.

He was right. It took four hours to recount my entire story, from beginning to end. This was the first time I had ever told it in its entirety to anyone. The experience was both devastating and liberating. For the first time, the story was not mine alone to bear.

I had finally handed it over – not in fragmented pieces but as a complete narrative.

I realised that before this moment, I had always been selective about sharing the information, worried that it might be too much for my husband, siblings, parents, or friends to handle.

I had only given each person pieces of the puzzle, leaving me with a jumbled and incomplete picture.

This was the first time I felt I was in a situation where I could trust that the person receiving my story wouldn't be heartbroken by it. In fact, every detail I shared was met with understanding, which helped me recall memories I didn't even know I had.

For the first time, I used language that accurately described the abuse. I called the acts by their true names and faced all the facts and emotions that came with them.

Although some pieces of the picture were still missing, I was freed by the knowledge that the burden of completing this puzzle was no longer mine alone to bear.

In this process, it was crucial to get every detail correct. The police officer explained that cases had been lost because there was room for the defendant to claim something like, "She did not specify what it was in her mouth. It could have been anything."

Every detail mattered:

Where was his hand?

Where was your foot?

Where were you looking?

Did he have a belt?

Which side was it unbuckled on?

Was it cold?

What were you wearing?

How did he get you to the bathroom?

Did he ask you to go, or did another adult ask him to take you?

Did he follow you?

These precise details could be the difference between conviction and acquittal at trial, if we make it that far. I remember feeling that little voice inside me worry that I would get in trouble for not having all the answers.

I couldn't recall everything – it was so long ago – but the memories that stood out were clear. I could describe the cake at my party. I could tell you the colour of the slide. I could even detail that the bathroom had two cubicles, because I felt as though I was floating above them. I left my body when he was hurting me, as it was too much for my little mind to comprehend. In those moments, I would disconnect to survive.

My mind, my soul, my pride, my higher self – I'm still trying to understand who or what left, but I know that detaching from my body was a survival tool and allowed me to still have joy in my life. This wasn't all of me hurt, this was one small part. This disconnection kept me sane for a while, until it didn't. It allowed me to distance myself from those horrifying events just enough to still blow out the candles on my cake, even though those acts had stolen my breath and innocence.

I lacked the words to describe the abuse; the confusion was too overwhelming, so I locked it all away, much like I did with the birthday presents from my great aunts that were too babyish, not fit for a big girl turning five.

I put them out of sight at the back of my cupboard, like this event never existed in the first place. Recalling these details was piecing together fragments of memory.

I could describe the party, the cake, the ducks, but the most crucial details about the abuse often felt fragmented and out of reach. It was frustrating, almost as if there were parts of me still protecting those memories, locked away in an emotional vault. These gaps haunted me, making the process of recounting everything even more daunting.

Dissociation is a peculiar and profound mechanism, a silent guardian that some survivors of sexual assault employ to navigate the treacherous waters of extreme trauma. It manifests in myriad ways, each a unique path through the labyrinth of the mind, designed to block out or disconnect from the harsh reality of the assault. For me, it was like an out-of-body experience.

Imagine standing outside a darkened room, your own body ensconced within its shadowy depths. From the hallway, you watch. The detachment is surreal, a necessary shield that allows you to separate from the agony inside that room. It's as though you are a silent observer, rather than the one enduring the torment. As a result, memory gaps follow, like a torn photograph with pieces scattered in the wind. Recollections of the event become hazy, fragmented. Important details blur and vanish, creating a jigsaw puzzle with parts perpetually missing.

In parts, dissociation plunges into amnesia, like a thick fog rolling in, swallowing the landscape whole. Significant aspects of the assault vanish into this mist, forgotten. You find yourself unable to recall essential details, or sometimes, the entire event is blocked out for long periods. The fog is both a curse and a solace, hiding the horror but also the truth.

Through these diverse forms of dissociation, the mind carves paths of survival, weaving through the dark corridors of memory and emotion. Each twist and turn are a defence, a way to endure

the unendurable. It took years of healing and reading to understand that in moments of extreme danger, especially during
childhood, dissociation can be a crucial survival mechanism. It
allows a person to focus on immediate safety rather than on emotional processing, both physically and mentally.

For so long, I was angry at myself, instead of honouring the
incredible innovation of my body, mind, and spirit, which collectively helped me survive the abuse I experienced.

In the echo of memory, the curtain pattern weaves,
Recalling the layout of the house, silence grieves.
The bed I lay upon, the room at the back,
The window to the yard, a haunting track.

The scent of cigarettes and alcohol in the air,
A chilling reminder of a time spent in despair.
But in the shadows of silence, the question remains,
Did he utter words, or was it silence, that stains.

Three decades later, a conversation unfolds,
Unveiling the truth, the story it holds.
The tone, the confidence, the arrogance so stark,
No need for words, just intentions dark.

He knew, with certainty, the role you would play,
A good girl, compliant, in the silence you'd stay.
For the sake of others, for the peace to hold tight,
Your voice suppressed, hidden from sight.

In the echoes of silence, a tale untold,
Of strength and resilience, as you unfold.
Breaking free from the chains of the past,
Finding your voice, reclaiming my truth at last.

The Witness Statement

I took a deep breath as I entered the modestly furnished room. I have always been strong – for my two children, for my clients, for myself. But on this day, I felt vulnerable, a raw nerve exposed to the world. My hands trembled as I sat down across from the detective, who appeared both kind and stern, prepared for the difficulty of the conversation that lay ahead.

"Thank you for coming in, Kath," the detective began, his voice steady but soft. "I know this isn't easy, but your bravery is incredibly important. We need to go through everything in detail, and it's going to take some time. Are you ready?"

I nodded, my voice caught somewhere between a whisper and a sigh. I was ready, or at least as ready as I would ever be. It had taken me 23 years to muster the courage to walk into this room and recount the horrors I had locked away in the deepest parts of my memory.

The clock on the wall seemed louder than usual, each tick a reminder of the hours stretching ahead. I began to speak, the words coming slowly at first, as if each one must be wrestled free from my past.

I described the first incident – where it happened, who was there, what was said. I spoke about the park, the noises, the overwhelming fear that had consumed my young self. The parts that are blank, the parts that don't make sense.

The detective listened intently, occasionally interrupting to ask for clarification or to delve deeper into certain aspects. "Can you confirm the location of his hand, Kath?" he asked, making sure to document every haunting detail with precision.

Each question felt like a needle prick, forcing me to relive moments I had tried desperately to forget.

There was a brief pause after the first hour, allowing me to sip some water and gather my thoughts. The detective knew these breaks were crucial for my mental and emotional stamina.

When we resumed, I continued, describing the second incident. My voice found a rhythm, a cadence that matched the terrible drumbeat of my memories. This time, the detective focuses on the specifics – dates, times, the sequence of events.

"Let's go over that part again, just to be sure," the detective said gently. The repetition is necessary, but it is also an agonising reminder of the trauma I have endured.

By the third hour, fatigue was setting in. My eyes grew weary, the emotional weight of my story bearing down on me like a storm cloud. The detective paused again, offering me a moment to breathe. He assured me that we were making progress, that each minute spent is a step towards justice.

In the fourth hour, we moved to the third incident.

This is the hardest one for me to talk about. The details are seared into my mind, but speaking to them aloud feels like tearing open wounds that had taken decades to scar over.

I described every aspect – how the room looked, the pattern on the lace curtains. The overwhelming sense of helplessness, confusion, so much confusion.

My voice wavered as I recounted the final moments of that third incident. The room fell silent, except for the scribbling of the detective's pen and the ticking clock. I could see the empathy in his eyes, but I knew he must remain impartial, focused on gathering every piece of my story with unwavering accuracy.

"Kath, I know this is hard, but I need to ask you to confirm the sequence of events one more time," the detective said. His voice is firm yet kind, a reflection of his understanding of the immense courage it takes for me to be here.

The last hour was the most gruelling. The detective went over everything we had discussed, piece by piece, asking for confirmation and ensuring nothing had been missed. I felt my strength waning, but I pushed through, knowing this was a crucial step towards justice not only for myself, but for my children. They deserve a mother who has faced her past and fought for her future.

When the four-hour session finally ended, I was emotionally and physically drained. My body ached from the tension, my voice hoarse from the continuous recounting. But there was also a sense of relief, a glimmer of hope that maybe, just maybe, sharing my story in such excruciating detail had moved me one step closer to healing.

The detective stood up, giving me a respectful nod, his eyes filled with an understanding that transcends words. "Thank you,

Kath," he says softly. "Your strength is remarkable. We will do everything we can to ensure your story leads to justice."

As I left the police station, the weight of my memories still pressed upon me, but there was also a newfound lightness in my step – a testament to the power of confronting the past head-on. The ordeal had not broken me; it had given me the strength to seek justice not just for myself, but as a beacon for others who might be suffering in silence.

Each step I took away from the police station was a step towards reclaiming my life, piece by piece. I got to the car and when I received a text asking how I went, I responded with this poem that poured out of me.

I've told my story; I've said it all,
I have no control now how hard you might fall.
But you will know I have told my truth,
That you stole my innocence and impacted my youth.
Everything about my being is shaped by your acts,
But haven't taken my strength, my capacity to react.
The incidents happened, it accelerated my growth,
The healing that I have done created faith and hope.
You took something that should never have been taken,
But I am stronger than you and that can't be shaken.
Today I feel lost and sad and confused,
But the police have my story and this truth they will use.
My statement will lead to your inevitable arrest,
My time to stand up and your time to unrest.
My time to impart humiliation on you now,
No more questioning or understanding the how.

This is your strength to be tested this time,
Your vulgarness and actions yours to define.
Regardless of how far this investigation goes,
It's not our secret anymore, for just you and I to know.
Time for the world to see who you really are,
For you to know I had the strength to take it this far.
Time for you to face all you did to me,
Time for me to step up to all I can be.
I'm handing it over to the universe to take it from here,
I'm standing into my true self the memories I no longer fear.

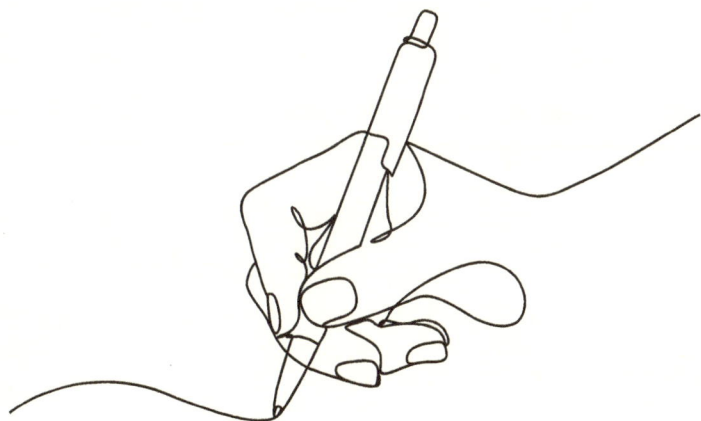

Detective Two

The female detective assigned to my investigation was on the verge of maternity leave, preparing for the profound journey of bringing a new life into the world. Observing her during this deeply personal and professional intersection, I couldn't help but marvel at the paradox she embodied. Here was a woman navigating the harrowing complexities of her job while on the brink of the transformative experience of motherhood.

As I watched her, questions swirled in my mind. How did she reconcile the demands and emotional toll of her work with the nurturing responsibilities of being a parent? Was she already familiar with the intricate dance of juggling career and family? Had she navigated these murky waters before, or was she about to step into the uncharted territory of first-time parenthood?

When I had my own daughter, a shift occurred in my perception of the world. The news, with its relentless stream of tragedies and injustices, became almost unbearable to watch. It was as if a new lens had been placed over my eyes – a lens tinted with urgency and vigilance, coloured by the instinct to protect at all costs. Every story of harm and suffering resonated with a newfound intensity, each incident a troubling reminder of the dangers that lurk in the shadows.

With motherhood came an overwhelming desire to shield my child from the world's cruelties. How could I ensure her safety in a world so fraught with danger? How could I become the kind of parent who would prevent history from repeating itself, sparing my child from the pain I endured?

These thoughts must surely have crossed the mind of the detective too, whose exposure to human suffering was magnified by her role. How did she manage to compartmentalise the darkness she encountered daily in her professional life and still foster a sense of security and optimism for her own child? Her strength and resilience in facing these dual realities became a source of immense admiration for me.

A pregnant detective, facing such strife,
Working on cases that cut like a knife.
Bringing a child into a world so dark,
Where innocence is shattered, leaving its mark.

Each day for you a battle, a war to be fought,
Knowing the dangers that each case has brought.
Seeing the pain that children endure,
It's a heavy burden, of that, I am sure.

Yet with each challenge, each heartbreaking view,
Comes a determination to fight for what's true.
To protect the vulnerable, to bring them light,
To stand against darkness, with all of your might.

So, the detective comes to work each and every day,
Carrying the weight of the cases that lay.
But with a heart filled with courage and grace,
Striving to create a safer, kinder place.

Birth

I am told my entry into the world was an ordeal – 37 hours of gruelling labour. This experience has frequently made me ponder – what does this say about me? My mother often describes those 37 hours as an exercise in determination and perseverance.

Her strength and resilience through such an extended and taxing labour process have always been a source of fascination and admiration for me. It makes me wonder if, in some way, my own nature was being foreshadowed by that challenging birth.

The stubbornness it took to endure such a protracted labour is something I see reflected in my own life and personality. Just like my birth, I often find myself pushing through difficulties with a blend of tenacity and endurance, refusing to give up until I reach my goals.

From an early age, I was always told that I was a 'good girl'. My mother would often recount how I slept through the night at just six weeks old, ate everything that was given to me, and was generally a happy, easy baby.

This makes me wonder: was I intrinsically this way, or did I somehow sense that I had already caused my mother so much pain during my birth that I strived to be less of a burden afterward? Could my easy-going nature have been an early manifestation of my determination to make things right, to ease the toll I had taken, even before I understood the concept?

my birth story

A 37-hour labour, a journey so long,
A test of endurance, a test so strong.
What does it say about the child being birthed?
What traits and characteristics are unearthed?
Perhaps it speaks of patience and grace,
A willingness to wait, to embrace,
The challenges that come with time.
To persevere through the mountain climb,
To push through the pain, to never give up,
To rise above, to drink from triumph's cup.
A 37-hour labour, a trial of might,
A child born after a fierce fight.
What does it say about your character, dear one?
That you are strong, that you have won.
Embrace the journey that brought you here,
For it has shaped you, it has made you clear.
You are a warrior, a fighter through and through,
A beacon of strength, a light that shines true.

my children's birth stories

Two births, two worlds apart,

Shaping me, shaping my heart,

With my daughter, a dreamlike scene,

Peace and serenity, a moment serene.

In warm water, to calming music's tune,

Quick and peaceful, under the sun and the moon.

A primal strength, a bond so deep,

A radiant glow, wisdom to keep.

Then came my son, a laborious tale,

Emotions heavy from a stormy gale,

Following miscarriages, grief in the air,

His arrival demanding fierce care.

No easy path, but determination strong,

Love overwhelming, relief after so long,

Transformative, deepening my motherhood bond,

Through the struggles, a love so fond.

My daughter, calm and composed alike,

Mirroring her birth, a peaceful strike.

While my son, with energy and curiosity wild,

Reflects the storm we faced, together compiled.

Evidence

Friends were interviewed, as they were the first people I told when my memories surfaced, that day back in Melbourne between the two weekends of wedding celebrations.

I still remember the day that I called my best friends; they were together on the other end of the phone when I reached out to tell them about the memories that had suddenly resurfaced. I shared with them how this resurfacing was the root cause of my ongoing depression over the past months, why I felt as if I was sinking into quicksand, unable to make sense of my reality any longer.

This revelation made sense as to why I had struggled to feel happiness despite having many reasons to be grateful. It was as though a hidden piece of my life's puzzle had finally clicked into place, making sense the fears and relationship difficulties I had carried for so long. The abuse had always been there, buried in my subconscious, influencing my life in ways I couldn't understand until those memories broke through the surface. My friends were supportive that day, their compassion helping me find some stability amid the chaos.

Family members were also interviewed to validate my story. They provided context and corroboration based on their observations and past events.

One specific incident that stood out was when I was taken to the hospital in pain after the abuse occurred when I was 11.

I don't remember much from that hospital visit, except the relief everyone felt when the diagnosis was a urinary tract infection and nothing more serious.

The acknowledgment of this hospital visit served as critical pieces of evidence supporting my claims. It became clear that my pain and struggles were deeply rooted in an abuse incident that had left a profound impact on my psyche and physical wellbeing.

As the investigation continued, the pieces of my past were painstakingly pieced together, helping to bring clarity to this lifelong battle with unexplained fears and depression.

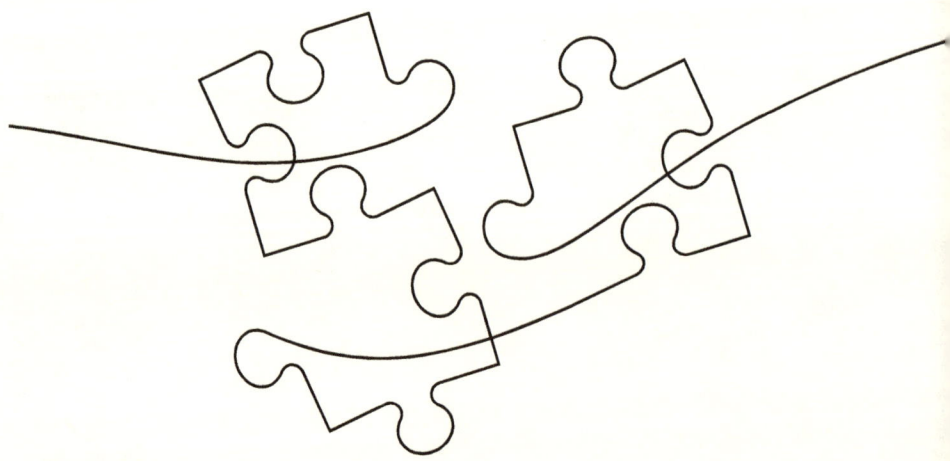

Why didn't they inquire about what occurred?
Why didn't I speak up, feeling so blurred?
Did they examine me down there at all?
Did they understand my pain wasn't from a fall?
Why didn't they inquire about what occurred?
Why didn't I speak up, feeling so blurred?
He crept into my bed the night before,
Feeling scared, feeling alone, at my core.
Why didn't I tell them, why didn't they see?
The truth behind my pain, the reality.

Layers of Trauma

My trauma was multifaceted, unfolding in distinct layers that intertwined to shape my reality. The first layer was the incidents of abuse – a sequence of painful events that tore at the fabric of my being, leaving scars that lingered long after the wounds had healed. These experiences etched a shadow on my soul, a haunting reminder of the darkness I had endured.

The second layer was the surfacing, the remembrance, the ghost of the past that haunted my present. Flashbacks and triggers would transport me back to moments of terror and helplessness, pulling me into a vortex of fear and despair. These memories had a corrosive power, eroding the fragile sense of peace I had tried so hard to maintain.

The third layer was the depression that followed, a heavy cloak of darkness that wrapped around my heart and suffocated my spirit. It whispered lies of unworthiness and isolation, feeding on the doubts and insecurities that festered within me. It was a relentless foe, sapping the joy from my days and casting a shadow on my every thought.

Despite the weight of these burdens, I had always felt like an outsider, a passerby in a world where I struggled to belong. It was a persistent feeling, a nagging voice that whispered of my difference from those around me. This sense of otherness led me to hide a significant part of myself, a vulnerable core that I shielded from prying eyes, afraid of rejection or judgement.

Paradoxically, while I harboured these hidden insecurities, I found solace in the company of others. I excelled in social situations, effortlessly connecting with people and making them feel valued and seen. It was a skill honed from years of masking my own vulnerabilities, a defence mechanism that allowed me to navigate the complexities of human interaction with ease.

As time passed, however, the cracks in my facade began to show. The trauma I carried within me crept into every aspect of my being, overshadowing the vibrant parts of myself that others admired. The happier, outwardly confident persona I presented to the world started to crumble, revealing the shattered fragments of my true self beneath the surface.

The more I tried to suppress this darker side of me, the more it demanded recognition, threatening to consume me whole. The unresolved trauma from the abuse became a central piece of my identity, a shadow that loomed large and unignorable. It was a pivotal moment in my journey towards healing, a reckoning with the demons that had haunted me for so long.

As I delved deeper into the complexities of my trauma, I realised that the abuse was just one element of a larger puzzle. Remembering and acknowledging these painful experiences became crucial in understanding the intricate dynamics at play within me. It explained the perpetual sense of disconnection I felt, the inner desolation that contrasted sharply with the external facades of love and friendship.

The internal conflict I grappled with was profound, a clash between the vibrant persona I projected to the world and the fragile, broken core I harboured within. I lived in a dual reality, outwardly engaging yet inwardly wounded, oscillating between moments of connection and profound isolation. As I excavated the layers of my past, the pervasive impact of the trauma became illuminated. It touched every fibre of my being, reshaping my perceptions, beliefs, and relationships.

The investigation into my abuse peeled back the layers of my existence, revealing the raw vulnerability that lay beneath the surface. This journey towards self-discovery was arduous and painful, but it was also liberating. It lifted the veil of confusion and self-doubt, shedding light on the reasons behind my persistent feelings of alienation and loneliness. By confronting the depths of my trauma, I embarked on a path towards wholeness and healing, embracing the complexities of my past as integral to my present journey of growth and resilience.

In the depths of my soul, layers of pain reside,
Each one a chapter in the story I hide,
Step one, abuse, a darkness that lingers,
The echoes of cruelty, the touch of cold fingers.

Step two reveals the resurfacing of memories,
A flood of emotions, like turbulent seas,
The past breaches the dam, the truth breaks through,
Unearthing the wounds I thought I outgrew.

Step three is the aftermath, the aftermath of it all,
Reclaiming shattered pieces, answering the call,
Reconfiguring my soul in the face of the black,
Navigating the shadows, can no longer go back.

Each layer a burden, each step a trail,
Through trauma's intricate web, I slowly sail,
In the darkness, a light begins to gleam,
A flicker of hope in the layers unseen.

I unravel the threads that bind me tight,
Confronting the darkness, embracing the light,
For in the layers of trauma, I find my strength,
A survivor's journey, no matter the length.

Dad

My dad was a good man, and I have many happy memories of him from my childhood. He loved me deeply and always made me feel cherished. He had an infectious sense of humour that could light up any room, and he was well-liked by everyone who knew him. His generosity was boundless, and he would give the shirt off his back to help someone in need. Despite his many wonderful qualities, my dad had his flaws. He was often lazy, and in hindsight, I can see that he lacked emotional intelligence at times.

I always felt like I had a certain wisdom beyond my years, an intuitive understanding of emotions and situations that he seemed to lack. It felt as if I was born with this innate sense of empathy and insight. Because of this, our roles often felt reversed; I frequently felt like I was the parent in our relationship. I was the one offering support, being the wise and understanding figure.

I vividly remember the day my parents told us they were breaking up. I was eight years old, and my brother was six. They sat us down for this life-altering conversation and then cleverly distracted us by ordering takeout for dinner. Even at that young age, I recognised the tactic and thought it was quite ingenious. It helped to shift our focus away from the painful revelation, if only for a little while.

After my dad moved out, he took my brother and me to see Santa in the city. It was a special outing meant to lift our spirits before Christmas. On the way, we stopped at a church to light a candle and say a prayer. My dad asked us to pray for him and Mum to get back together. I have never asked my brother what he prayed for, and I still don't know to this day. But I remember clearly, I prayed for a Cabbage Patch doll.

I had a conversation with God, though, and explained that I knew it was a waste of a wish to ask for my parents to reunite. That it felt weird to be here lighting a candle when it was the first time dad had ever taken us to do that before. In my young mind, it seemed so impossible for things to ever be better between them. I felt like I just knew, deep down, that it would be better if Dad wasn't living with us anymore.

This intuitive sense of understanding, even at such a young age, has stayed with me throughout my life. It shaped my relationship with my dad and my view of my family. Despite his shortcomings, I always knew he loved me and wanted the best for us, even if he didn't always know how to show it.

As I experienced my own bouts of depression, I began to wonder if this was what it was like for him too – hiding from those around him because he couldn't face his internal struggles, whatever that looked like for him.

He wasn't a heavy drinker like my abuser, but food was his addiction. I always knew if I wanted a treat, he was the parent to ask. That's how I learnt the rules of football – I would watch his reactions to the game, figuring out the right moment to say I was hungry. Waiting for a pivotal moment in the game, I'd say, "Dad, I'm hungry. I've finished all the food Mum packed for us. Can I buy something now?"

He would hand over whatever was in his wallet without looking and keep watching the game. "Yes, get me one too," he would say. Winning! A hot jam donut, just like that! But life became more complicated as I got older; the heaviness in my body grew more pronounced.

I was told once that my nanna would spend days in bed at a time.

Why? Was I like her? Was I like my dad? Or was this the result of intergenerational unsolved trauma? Would I ever know? Did I need to know?

My perspective around my own depression was shaped by watching my dad fall further and further from the happy-go-lucky guy I knew and loved. He became a victim of everything – his job, his ex-wife, his newest ex-wife, his health, his children being taken from him, losing his relationship with his children because he was forced to move up to QLD away from us.

His conversations were dominated by 'what ifs' and 'not fairs', which was exhausting and saddening.

Was this really who I was – a product of this sad man with no family and no real future? Was this what I was destined for, a product of a family full of secrets and pain? Was this all I could hope for in my future relationships and happiness?

I remember when I qualified for states in swimming after training for 18 months.

"Careful, no boy will go out with a girl who has bigger shoulders than them," they joked. I remember when I first got into university to study Teaching. "Well, that will be a waste of time," they said, "there are no jobs for teachers."

My nanna wasn't like that. She loved me for all that I was and all I was becoming. She would secretly ask me how my mum was and tell me to say "hi" to her. "Don't tell your dad," she would say.

I felt loved by her because she seemed to see all of me – both sides – the parts made up from my mum and my dad, or more specifically, from her. I related to her more than anyone in that side of the family. She was positive, fun, lively, and the life of the party every time. She was tiny, just 4'5", but had fiery red hair and a huge personality, always able to make me smile. She would make my brother and me sugar sandwiches on white bread with heaps of butter.

She was a cooking teacher, and I remember being out with her once when a few of her students said hello. I wanted to be like her when I grew older – always hosting parties and bringing people together. I had to find the good in this half of myself. I couldn't be made up of just depression, sadness and dysfunction.

We are both here,
But we are completely alone.

Guilt

I felt immense guilt walking away from half of my family. When my memories resurfaced in my twenties, I knew I would have to tell my dad what happened. Unlike with my mum and her extended family, I knew that he wouldn't be capable of supporting me, and I knew it would change things and cause him pain.

For that, I felt more guilt. Why didn't I remember earlier? What if something happened to someone else, and I could have stopped it?

Deep guilt.

My brother and I made the difficult decision to distance ourselves from our entire extended family. My brother tried to fill the supportive role that our dad never could.

Because I was living in Darwin when my memories surfaced, he moved there to be near me, ensuring I wasn't alone. I am his big sister; he shouldn't have to look after me. Guilt. We faced our parents' divorce together, and we navigated living in two homes.

He was the only person who truly understood the difficulty of not being able to play sports on the weekends because of having to stay with our dad every second weekend; you can't commit to a team if you're only available half the time. We both shared a mutual sorrow for our dad's downfall and his inability to step up when it mattered. However, I believe it was harder on my brother – the disappointment cut deeper for him. Boys need their dads.

On my return home, surrounded by friends and family, my guilt was still present. On a journey to the snow, my friends and I made a stop to pick up some refreshments for the road. I dashed into a pub, intending to buy drinks to take with us, but before I even entered the bar, I was stopped by an unexpected sight – my dad and my abuser casually sharing a beer together.

In that moment, all the scenarios I had envisioned of confronting my abuser came crashing down. Never had I envisioned my father, complicit in camaraderie with him at the time. I couldn't do that to my dad, he wouldn't cope. More guilt. Without a second thought, I turned and left the pub before either of them had the chance to notice me.

Ironically, a profound sense of relief washed over me. At this point, I hadn't spoken to my dad in six years. So much guilt. But seeing them together had a way of clearing a new path and moving away from the guilt that I had harboured about our severed relationship. If he could comfortably socialise with the person who had inflicted such pain upon me after I confided in him, then I was absolved from feeling guilty about keeping him out of my life.

Staggered, I called my mum to share what had just occurred. I remember speaking with a sense of awe, amazed by the odd chance of the encounter, but now as I recount this, I can't help but question how that image, that piece of news, must have incited anger and distress in my mother and brother when they heard about it.

To me, it felt like a gift, a weight lifted. The guilt was gone.

I am sorry that I was hurt by someone you love,
I am sorry that you are struggling to rise above.

As the father, the protector, the one who should fight,
Why do I carry this guilt, the burden so tight?

I am the child, the one who was abused,
The pain, the trauma, the scars left bruised.

You, the father, the one I trusted so dear,
Where was the fight, the love, the shield, the spear?

I am the one going through this storm,
The one left shattered, broken, and torn.

Yet the weight of guilt on me heavy and strong,
Why do I carry it, why with me does it belong?

I am the daughter, seeking solace and peace,
In a world where the scars refuse to release.

I yearn for the strength, the love, the embrace,
From the father whose warmth I seek to retrace.

You can't fight for me, that much is clear,
But this guilt I can't bear, so let it disappear.

Acceptance

In our journey of healing, it's a messy path to navigate. There are days when mistakes are made, when partners may not know how to support, when friends are unsure how to help, and when siblings or parents may lack the tools to provide the necessary guidance. I have faced and overcome all of these challenges.

My path was far from smooth; it was a rough track where I often felt lost in the wilderness, struggling to express my needs and emotions. It's important to remember that past trauma can trigger fight, flight, or freeze responses. I personally experienced all of these at different times.

As I reflect back on my journey, there was a significant moment in my twenties when I returned from Darwin. My closest friends staged an intervention, urging me to overcome my struggles and get back on my feet.

They believed in my strength and ability to move forward, even though they lacked the full understanding of my situation. While their intentions came from a place of love and concern, I realised that the path to healing was unique to me.

Because they hadn't lived it, I hadn't shared it all so their advice was only coming from the Kath that I had shown them up until that point. This Kath was not all of me, but she was the part of me that had to be faced to overcome the trauma.

Despite their heartfelt advice, I knew deep down that I was capable of overcoming the darkness within me and becoming the person I aspired to be. It was a bumpy mountain bike track, filled with obstacles like rocks, trees, and mud, but with perseverance and self-awareness, I could find my way back to the light.

It was a complicated path for my mum and I, both strong individuals but very different in how we approach health and wellbeing. There was a period of time when our differences meant we didn't speak for months, causing her pain, for which I am sorry, as I know she struggled with not having all the right answers.

We sought the help of a counsellor to facilitate understanding between us, a pivotal moment in our relationship. After a couple of months of fortnightly sessions, we reached a breakthrough during the final session. Frustrated, my mother implored me to express my needs, "Tell me what you need Kath, and I will give it to you," leading to a flood of tears from me.

The counsellor intervened, explaining to my mum that my five-year-old self was struggling, unable to articulate what I needed. She was the one stuck, without her needs being met, not Kath in her forties sitting here today.

As I collected myself, I shared with her that there was a pivotal moment from my fifth birthday when, after experiencing abuse, I walked from the public toilet and straight to her. In that moment I didn't tell her what had happened, I simply told her that I wanted to go home.

Reflecting on this as a mother myself, I realised how children often struggle to express their true feelings. This revelation haunted me – I had never shared this vulnerable moment with my mum for fear of upsetting her, but not telling her was the wall that created a barrier between us. In this session, I finally revealed this experience to her, prompting her response of apology and understanding: "I am so sorry, Kath."

That acknowledgement was all I needed for my younger self to be validated and reminded that while there were times, she couldn't see my needs, there were countless moments where she did.

It was also freeing as a mother myself; I will not get it right all the time. I will, in fact, make thousands of mistakes while I do my best to support my children though the tides of forever-changing needs of childhood.

But being a good parent is not about when we have got it right or wrong, it is about continuing to show up., That is what my mum did for me that my father couldn't; she kept showing up even when there were times I didn't want her to.

That is what my friends have also done for me – showed up time and time again when it was my instinct to hide and push them away. There are friends who will never know that a simple text to check in saved me from an isolated moment of despair. The shame of new memories I wasn't ready to share was being carried on my own until I was ready to hand it over, but this was opening me a tiny piece at a time.

As a survivor, I expected so much from these people that loved me, without really sharing the whole picture. This is where we all need to accept that we are doing our best. We are doing our best to heal, and we need to trust that most people will be there as best they can to support you through it.

Acceptance in the messy ride is all we have; be kind to you and yours.

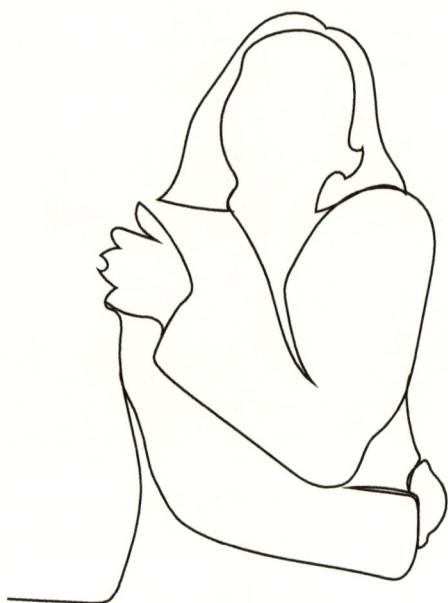

In the tapestry of healing, we find our way,
Accepting words we cannot say.
Embracing actions, where we may stray,
Navigating paths in our own sway.

Acceptance blooms in hearts so true,
Knowing we're all flawed, me and you.
Learning each day, a lesson anew,
Kindness our compass, forever in view.

For in acceptance, we find our grace,
In flaws and virtues, we find our place.
Growing and learning, at our own pace,
Embracing kindness, in life's embrace.

Chapter Five

Detective Three

During the birth of my daughter, I received unwavering support. The first midwife was gentle and patient, guiding me through the challenges of childbirth. Just when I needed it, the next midwife arrived, assertive and strong enough to push me forward.

During the investigation, I sensed a similar occurrence. As detective number two left to have her baby, I was introduced on the phone to detective three.

He seemed younger, but like the female detective, I never had the chance to meet him in person, with our only interactions over the phone. Reflecting on the absence of video calls, I'm curious, was this ever offered as an option? I strongly prefer visual options, but I can't recall if anyone presented them.

Despite the uncertainties, I carried on, following instructions, meeting expectations, and focusing on each task, one step at a time. It was all about moving forward and tackling the next challenge at hand.

Detective three played a crucial role; he was supportive, and I felt genuine care from him. When he transitioned to another department, he took the time to send me an email detailing victim compensation opportunity. Despite the offer of financial restitution, my motivations for pursuing justice weren't about monetary compensation. How could you even quantify that? The time, energy, and resources I dedicated to my healing journey were immeasurable, and no sum of money could erase the pain and suffering inflicted upon me.

I viewed my healing as a profound learning experience. Some might say it was a spiritual contract agreed upon before my birth, with lessons to be carried over into future lifetimes. Finding purpose in suffering was the way to make sense of it all.

While I grappled with these theoretical questions, I couldn't help but reflect on the impact of trauma and the cycle of pain it perpetuates. I questioned the motives behind my abusers' actions, pondering the unresolved trauma that may have driven him to commit such atrocities.

The deep-rooted trauma within my family, hinted at by my father's cryptic response upon learning about my abusers' actions, opened a Pandora's box of inquiries delving into the complex dynamics of generational trauma and its effects.

My dad's nonchalant response and his unwavering love and care for me left me grappling with conflicting emotions and unanswered questions. Was the trauma so ingrained in the fabric of our family history that it shaped the destinies of its members in contrasting ways?

Despite the perplexing nature of these familial dynamics, one thing remained steadfast: the awareness that the cycle of trauma had to be broken, and I would do everything I could to keep my own children safe.

Detective three contacted another relative who witnessed my abuse when I was 11. This detective emailed me just prior to his four rostered days off work. The email mentioned the witness being defensive, uncooperative, and making accusations about another male relative.

'Let's discuss when I return from my break,' the email said.

Another relative? Who? I spiralled.

Eventually, after many panicked messages being left and emails sent, the phone rang. It was detective three.

"Who" I said, "Who was it she accused?" I burst into tears. Desperately, I asked him if the relative in question was my dad. He reassured me it wasn't my dad, but another family member.

After finding out who, explaining that although this person had done nothing to me, he was someone I neither trusted nor liked, and I had always kept my distance from him.

The detective verified that the witness had no motive to lie and seemed upset during the call. Before hanging up, she had uttered a heartbreaking statement: "Where were you when I was a child?"

After that, her phone number got disconnected and the police couldn't locate her. *But weren't they the police?* I thought. *Couldn't they locate anyone?*

They couldn't force her to talk – not about her own abuse or what she witnessed happening to me. This was hard to process. Years of staying silent to protect her from having to speak up and further harm had just revealed there was more harm done, anyway. It broke my heart because I carried immense guilt for not speaking up earlier for her.

Now, she wasn't willing to help, which was fair enough, especially if she wasn't ready to confront her own trauma, leaving me wondering if confronting this earlier could have led to some semblance of happiness for both of us.

This new information really rattled me. What kind of family was this? Why is there so much happening without anyone discussing it?

I vividly remember being young at a Christmas gathering when my aunt, who was a nurse, was tending to my cousin's nails. My cousin had bitten them so low that they were bleeding. I kept thinking, *Can't they see what is happening? Can't they see how much pain she is in?* I could see it. Why not them? Why was no one helping her?

Although I didn't consciously comprehend what was happening, I knew she needed help; and I knew it was bad. Her biting her nails was clearly a cry for help that no one was listening to.

I had already lost the capacity to speak about my suffering, so these realisations left me feeling helpless and voiceless. In addition to this family's silence, there was an inability to notice the truth. I wondered how far back this stemmed and where it began.

How do you measure the worth of a soul,
Torn apart by trauma, trying again to become whole?
So, tell me, what is the price of my worth?
Of the battles fought, the healing unearthed.
No amount of money can truly equate,
To the value of a spirit that refuses to break.

Magic

The three incidents of abuse that shattered my sense of safety and security were like three strikes of lightning, leaving a lasting imprint of fear and doubt in my young mind. It was as if the very fabric of my reality had been torn apart, leaving me adrift in a sea of uncertainty and not knowing any other alternative. In the aftermath of these traumatic experiences, I found solace in the sanctuary of my imagination. I retreated into a world of magic and make-believe, where I could rewrite the script of my life and become the fearless protagonist of my own story.

In this fantastical realm, I was the master of my fate, able to vanquish any foe or obstacle that dared to threaten my newfound sense of empowerment. Navigating the complexities of childhood with a fractured sense of trust, I relied on my imagined reality as a lifeline, a refuge from the harsh realities of abuse that lurked just beyond the edge of my make-believe world.

The characters in my fantastical universe were not just figments of my imagination; they were allies and companions who walked by my side, offering comfort and support in times of need. I drew strength from the magic of my imagination, using it as a shield to protect myself from the harsh reality of trauma. The fairies and angels that danced in the corners of my mind were not just figments of my imagination; they were messengers of a deeper truth that I alone could comprehend.

Through the wisdom gleaned from the abuse, I had developed a heightened awareness, a sixth sense that guided me through the labyrinth of danger and uncertainty. There were moments when I could perceive things that others couldn't, a whisper of intuition that urged me to stay away from certain individuals, avoid certain places, or take a different path. It was as if I was being guided by an invisible hand, a force greater than myself that shielded me from harm and steered me towards safety.

This innate knowing was not born of fear or paranoia, but rather a profound sense of connection to a higher power, a cosmic force that watched over me with benevolent eyes. It was a feeling that ran deeper than mere superstition or fanciful belief; it was a bone-deep certainty that resonated within the very core of my being.

In moments of doubt and uncertainty, I drew strength from this unshakable faith, this unerring compass that guided me through the stormy seas. I embraced my gift with gratitude and humility. I knew that I was not alone in this world, that I was held in the loving embrace of something greater than myself.

In a world of shadows and fear,
My little girl found solace near,
Imagining fairies and angels so bright,
Guiding me through the dark of night.

When the world seemed cruel and unkind,
I'd close my eyes and leave it behind,
The pain and sorrow that filled my heart,
And in my dreams, a new world would start.

Fairies danced in fields of gold,
With magic wings that gently fold,
Angels whispered secrets divine,
Promising that everything would be fine.

In times of trouble, when the bad crept near,
She'd call upon her friends so dear,
Believing in the power of good and light,
Knowing that darkness couldn't win the fight.

Through her imagination, she found a way,
To keep the darkness at bay,
For in her world of make-believe,
The good would inevitably be achieved.

Pretext Call

The authorities never found the evidence of my hospital visit to support my investigation. This missing tangible proof made it challenging to build a concrete case. Without this crucial evidence, the authorities advised that, before formally arresting my abuser, I might consider making a phone call to see if he would confess.

"Pretext call" is the term used to refer to this type of phone call. The victim's goal during the call is to elicit incriminating statements or a confession from the abuser, which law enforcement can use as evidence in the investigation.

I was told that it was perfectly fine if I didn't feel up to making this call. They explained a pretext call could be a highly effective tool because it captures the abuser's words in an unguarded moment, potentially leading to an admission of guilt.

However, such calls can also be incredibly distressing and emotionally challenging for the victim, as they require direct interaction with the person who caused them harm. Pretext calls are helpful in situations where physical evidence is lacking or hard to get.

Investigators perform pretext calls to gather direct evidence through conversation, which can confirm the victim's account of events and strengthen the case against the abuser. Law enforcement typically provides guidelines on how to conduct the call safely and effectively.

As I contemplated this option, I weighed the emotional toll against the potential benefit of obtaining a confession. The thought of hearing his voice and possibly confronting him with the pain he had caused was daunting. However, the possibility that this call could significantly help the case and prevent future abuse was a compelling reason to consider it.

In that crucial moment, my 11-year-old self screamed yes, and her voice guided me this time.

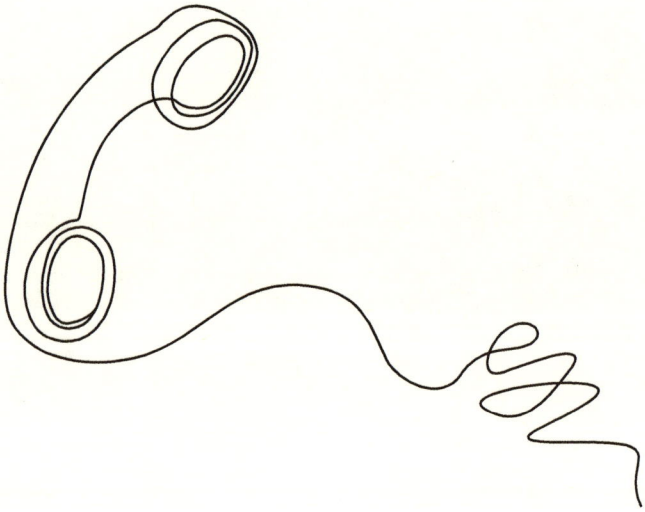

In a world of shadows, where echoes fade,
A phone call stands, in moments made.
No evidence found, a challenge faced,
A victim's courage, about to be encased.

A 'pretext call' in the silence rings,
Seeking truth where the darkness clings.
A victim's strength, a choice profound,
To confront the past on uncharted ground.

Emotions raw, the memories stir,
Facing the abuser, a mind a whir.
But in the balance, a voice emerged,
Guiding the path where justice surged.

Through the fear and doubt that creep,
A decision made in moments deep.
The young self within, resolute and clear,
Said yes to the call, in courage sincere.

Before the Call

When I entered the small room at the police station, I encountered an atmosphere thick with nervous anticipation. The officer handed me a piece of paper, and I noticed a slight tremor in my hand. The document acknowledged that I would be alone in the room during the call, acting of my own free will and without coercion.

My eyes fell on my abuser's number printed on the paper.

Nausea surged through me as I saw the number in my phone. Just looking at it triggered a flood of painful memories. Deleting his number was the first thing I needed to do after this ordeal. I wanted no connection, nothing to link me back to the trauma he had caused.

I thought I would make the call from the police phone. Could he trace it back to me? Would he see it? How could I ensure he wouldn't? Panic rose within me, but I had to stay calm for the little girl inside me's sake. I reassured myself that I had this under control, and it would be fine. However, the use of my phone threw me off.

The officer, whom I had never met before, was abrupt and distant. The only information about me that she knew was written on that piece of paper – his name and number, my name and number, all on the same page.

This in itself felt like a violation.

When she left the room and handed me the recording device, I feared messing it up. What if it didn't work? What if all this effort proved futile? My fears swirled.

It was during another Covid lockdown in Victoria, and my husband was at home, homeschooling the children. The officer showed me how to change my number to a private one. I did as instructed, but anxiety plagued me.

What if he saw my number? What if I got that part wrong and he could contact me? It was too much to consider.

I called my husband; no answer. I texted, "It's me, Kath. Is this my number or a private one?" I called again before he could respond. "No caller ID, Kath. Are you okay?" he asked. "Yes, I have to go. Thank you."

I had given little thought to the possibility of hearing his voice. I was preoccupied with his potential response. Would he cry and apologise, his remorse clear in every word? If he did, what could I do with that apology?

Could it ever mend the wounds he inflicted? Or would he deny everything, calling me a liar, adding another layer of hurt to what I already carried? Would he simply hang up, avoiding confrontation entirely? And what if, despite the anticipation, he ignored the call? The uncertainty was overwhelming.

To prepare, I had visited a psychotherapist twice that week, seeking strength and assurance. I needed to ensure that, at this critical moment, my voice wouldn't betray me. I aimed for the strongest parts of my character to emerge, unbreakable and unwavering.

That morning, at 9:30 am, a group of supportive individuals held a meditation session for me. I could feel their collective energy, like a warm embrace of reassurance – like the magic I was comforted by as a child. Knowing that they were in a state of calm at that exact time, sending me their strength, was deeply moving. This shared tranquillity was especially necessary because the process had been delayed by 45 minutes, stretching my nerves even thinner.

My mantra, a steadfast companion in these moments, could only carry me so far. I needed to lean on others who were older, wiser, and more in touch with their truths than me that day. Or perhaps I was closer to my truth than I dared to believe. Despite my doubts, I knew I was ready for this call. I had to trust in the outcome, whatever it might be.

With trembling hands, I dialled his number.

Ring, ring; the sound echoed in the quiet room. It was 10:30 am.

Ring, ring; the passage of time felt surreal. It was a Tuesday.

Ring, ring; another snap lockdown in Victoria added to the surrealism.

Ring, ring; the phone displayed 'No Caller ID', anonymity I hoped would protect me.

Each ring felt like an eternity, the unnerving silence stretching on the other side.

He didn't answer. The call rang out, leaving me in a limbo of relief, frustration, and unanswered questions. In that prolonged silence, I felt a mixture of emotions. Relief washed over me, knowing I didn't have to confront him directly – at least, not today.

Frustration bubbled beneath the surface, as all my preparations seemed wasted. I feared the questions – those painful, lingering questions – would remain unanswered, chipping away at my restored peace I had worked so hard to connect with.

I sat there, reflecting on my experience during my daughter's birth, and surrendered to the moment in the same way. Just as my body had instinctively known what to do, I needed to let my heart take over, trusting in a higher power, in that instinct as a child I learnt to trust, in the magic that led me into the police station in the first place.

I took a deep breath. I felt supported, accepting that whatever was in my highest good would unfold. I decided in that moment that if he answered, it would lead to a path of peace; if he didn't, it might be too much for me to cope with.

I prayed fervently to the goddesses, the angels, God, and my departed family and friends, asking for healing to be the ultimate outcome of this next step regardless of the direction it took. I simply stepped aside, surrendered and let the universe work its magic.

In a room where shadows fade and light finds its way,
A journey unfolds, a voice seeks its say.
Sessions of healing, where hearts align,
A space held by love, a soul to entwine.

With courage as armour, the little girl within,
Embarks on a quest, a battle to win.
To find her voice, to speak her truth,
In a world where silence stole her youth.

Surrounded by energy, a meditative embrace,
A group of souls, sending love and grace.
Creating a sanctuary, where vulnerability thrives,
A safe haven where healing arrives.

Through the storms and the tears,
The little girl emerges, despite the pain and fears.
Her voice grows louder, her spirit set free,
In a circle of love, where she's meant to be.

And in this sacred space, where healing is found,
The little girl within, in love, is bound.
With each session, a step towards the light,
Guided by love, shining ever so bright.

Hello

I tried one more time. If he answered, it was meant to be; if he didn't, it wasn't. Once again, the phone started ringing.

Ring, ring; I am strong.

Ring, ring; I am safe.

Ring, ring; I am protected.

Ring, ring; I am guided.

Ring, ring – "Hello?"

He answered. The voiceless monster who had hurt me had a voice, and I recognised it immediately. Through therapy, I had remembered so much, but I had erased his voice from my memory, along with the words he used to keep me silent all those years ago.

How a single sound can trigger an instant flood of memories is peculiar. My initial reaction was physical – I felt the urge to run and hide. The scared part of me retreated.

Then my voice, the part waiting to reclaim itself, took control.

"Hello, it's Kathryn," I said, my voice trembling yet resolute. "I have some questions for you related to memories that have surfaced from my childhood."

I braced myself, expecting him to hang up and leave me in silence. Instead, he simply responded with, "Okay." In that moment, I felt a powerful mix of fear and empowerment. I began confronting my past directly to the only person who could answer the questions I needed answering.

In the depths of trauma, a silence profound,
No sound to recall, just feelings unbound.
Snippets of imagery, pain, and fear,
A haunting echo, not crystal clear.
Suffocation, pain, and a heavy weight,
Emotions stirred, a relentless freight.
But no sound to accompany the scenes,
A void in memory, shattered dreams.
Then his voice breaks through, sharp and clear,
A tsunami of reality, drawing near.
All it took was a simple hello,
To shatter the silence, to stir the flow.
A single word, a whisper creates fright,
Opening floodgates, revealing the night.

That Didn't Happen

The conversation lasted over ten minutes. Although it was being recorded for police evidence, that fact didn't influence the direction I took. I was putting the final puzzle pieces in place for me, not the police.

I asked him if he had recalled my birthday party at the park. His response was, "That didn't happen."

I asked if he remembered taking me to the bathroom at Easter. Again, he said, "That didn't happen."

His voice remained calm, his composure almost unnervingly steady. Surprisingly, he never gave me an opportunity to delve into the specifics of these incidents, he was so quick to deny. When I later pointed this out to the police, they nodded. "Good pick up," they said.

Then I queried him regarding the last incident, the only one with a witness. His response was the same: "That didn't happen."

But this time, I heard it, a tiny flicker of concern, a moment of uncertainty in his voice. The conversation ended as you might expect, with him trying to reclaim his power. But I had come way too far to let that happen today.

I ended the call by telling him:

"When I look in the mirror, I see a woman who knows her strength. That strength has been with me since I was a child. Now I see you are simply a man who tried to take it from me because you didn't have the capacity to reach deep inside yourself and find your own."

In those ten minutes, I had dissolved decades of pain, fear, and self-blame. Despite his attempt, I survived that phone call as I had survived the incidents of abuse.

You're alive, and we have spoken, and now I feel dead,
The pain inside of me swirling and I'm left with dread.
I can't grab a hold of what I'm supposed to feel,
My childhood was stolen, I see it now, it's real.
Hearing your voice and sensing your control,
The evil inside tried to penetrate my soul.
You have always been who I sense you to be,
The clarity of my hopelessness is evident to me.
You live in this evil; you grow inside here,
The little girl inside me crumbles down in fear.

Doubting her story because of your words,
Your bullying behaviour unravelling her nerves.
I can't take a breath; I can't get out of bed,
The pain has taken over my body; it feels full of lead.
How can you still be living, happy as can be?
Why did I have to leave after I told what you did to me?
You're all still one big family and I am on the outside,
You're living your life, and I am alone in bed trying to hide.
I fucking hate you, you piece of shit. I hope you rot in hell,
Will there ever be a day where you are thrown into a cell?

Four Days

I hung up the phone. Then I screamed. My body shook uncontrollably.

I went home and stayed in bed for four days. During that time, waves of grief, sadness, and anger washed over me. My sorrow extended beyond me; it affected the people I loved, those who supported me.

Four days of letting go, and then reality hit me. I felt lighter, clearer. I had told my story, and in doing so, I had reclaimed my power. This conversation was the missing piece of my puzzle.

It was then that I realised that the little five-year-old girl in me wasn't scared anymore. The eight-year-old wasn't on high alert. And the 11-year-old had stopped blaming herself for going to that sleepover with her cousin.

I know I need to write, but I don't know what to say,
I have been in and out of my body for several days.
I'm lost and hurt, and my pain is too much to feel,
Hearing his voice has made it all so real.
I know you're there for me if I only I could call,
Something stops me from reaching out, to get past it all.
He silenced me for 40 years, that is only half the fact,
Thinking it would be too much to hear is what held me back.
He raped me and I didn't tell the truth of what he did,
The pain is too much for me to feel, so from you the
truth I hid.
Can you hear it now? because it's time for me to speak,
I have been letting it all come out for just under a week.
I invite you now to call me up and for us to discuss the truth,
I know my past is behind me and I can't get back my youth.
But the future must be free of the hold it had on me,
Tomorrow must be lighter, it's time to become who I am
meant to be.

A New Day

Returning to my daily life felt different now. The world seemed brighter, full of possibilities that were previously shrouded in shadows. Joy resided in simple pleasures: friends' laughter, sun's warmth, good books. Not distractions anymore, but affirmations of life and resilience.

My relationships also experienced a shift. With my newfound clarity and strength, I could connect more deeply and honestly with the people I loved. There wasn't a story separating us anymore.

My husband and I had long, open conversations about my past and our future. My children saw a more present and joyful mother. My brother, who grieved along with me for walking away from our dad and his family, seemed lighter too. My healing was his healing. My friendships grew stronger, built on a foundation of authenticity and mutual support.

My voice had been found once again; I could ask for what I wanted. I felt a sense of worthiness, so it felt easier to ask. Every aspect of my life realigned.

I could feel my soul ignite with an intense passion as I merged my beloved career with the wisdom of resilience and empowerment. My creative outlets enabled me to express parts of myself that I had kept hidden for too long. In reclaiming my power, I not only freed myself from the grip of my past but also forged a path towards a future filled with hope and possibility.

The pieces of my life, once fractured, had come together to form a beautiful, intricate mosaic. Every piece, memory, and moment held significance, weaving a story of survival, strength, and triumph. As I moved forward, I carried with me the lessons of those ten minutes and the profound transformation they sparked.

During that journey, I encountered not just a survivor but a courageous warrior, able to face any challenge with grace. The conversation with my abuser was a defining moment, but it was just a part of a broader tapestry of healing and growth.

It confirmed my belief that my strength had always been within me, no matter how deeply buried. In facing him, I didn't just speak for the child I once was; I spoke for every part of myself that had endured and persevered.

As the chapters of my life continued to unfold, I found a new rhythm – a balance between acknowledging my past and living fully in the present. For my family, this journey has transformed our relationships. We've built new traditions based on open communication and mutual support. My children know me as both a mother and a survivor, someone who faced her fears and emerged stronger.

This authenticity has created a home filled with love, understanding, and vulnerability. An understanding that none of us will get it right all the time; love is about having patience for all shades of ourselves. I showed them my shadow constructively.

I went to bed and emerged like a butterfly, who had found her wings and was ready to fly. I simply paid attention to my inner self and heard her needs for the first time. I listened, and she rewarded me with a wholeness I had never experienced before.

Returning to life, a new light in my view,
Radiant possibilities, shadows bid adieu.
Simple joys bring wisdom, in laughter and sun,
Connections deepen, a journey begun.

Realigned in sync, passion and light ignite,
Hidden parts shine, in creative flight.
Empowered, reclaiming strength from the past,
Uniting the fragments, a mosaic vast.

Lessons learnt, a warrior in grace,
Shifting identity, past events embrace.
Healing and growth, a story unfolds,
Wings of courage, the future holds.

My children witness bravery, fears to face,
Love and understanding, a home's embrace.
In tranquillity and patience, all shades find,
Inner whispers heard, a wholeness binds.

Caterpillar's rest, butterfly's flight,
Listening within, a journey of light.
Embracing the past and present sheen,
A sense of wholeness, unforeseen.

The Arrest

Detective three clarified the specifics of my abuser's arrest. My abuser living in regional Victoria meant the detective had to wait for the right moment to travel because of the lockdown in Melbourne. I thought the police had the freedom to go anywhere, didn't they?

The arrest was the pivotal moment when they had accumulated enough evidence to interrogate him, and they were about to inquire about all the details I had shared with the police for months, processed for years, and endured for a lifetime.

Given the presumption of innocence until proven guilty, how would they respond and handle the situation? Is there any additional information about him that I will never know? Has he ever been accused of any wrongdoing? Has anyone else spoken up so far?

I remember the detective saying that he would make the arrest on Monday after spending Sunday night in regional Victoria.

Was my memory playing mind games with me, deceiving me?

He let me know over the phone that he had been questioned for three hours. *Three hours – good*, I thought.

He let me know that his life was filled with misery. Internally, I questioned what evidence this was based on exactly. I could have easily guessed that given his actions, miserable energy, and self-proclaimed alcoholism.

He strongly denied everything during the questioning and was shocked by the accusations. What a surprise.

At least he had a life-changing moment when a detective from Melbourne came to his town, arrested him in public, and interrogated him. I imagined this causing confusion and raising questions about his reputation in the community.

It's possible that this was simply the version I created in my mind. Did my mind fabricate all of this to give me closure?

I'm utterly confused about what really happened with this arrest. I received information about what occurred from detective three, or at least I thought I did. However, detective four's arrival shattered my comprehension of the case following his predecessor's sudden transfer to another division. Unintentionally, he illustrated an alternative version of the arrest.

As the situation persisted, the boundary between reality and imagination became unclear. With each new detective, I had to repeat my requests and stress the need for more details. I longed for better communication and responsiveness, understanding that waiting and speculating would only bring about frustration and anxiety.

My faith in the process crumbled due to a lack of communication, leaving me feeling more isolated than ever. Contrary to my belief, it was the local police officer, not detective three, who questioned my abuser.

I had hoped my abuser would feel a small part of the humiliation and pain he inflicted on me. I now have a new perspective on how the arrest played out in my mind.

Two men chat casually in a bar, holding beers as football plays in the background.

"Can we trust what she's claiming?" the policeman asked, with a beer in hand.

"That didn't happen," my abuser would respond.

The officer would respond, "Let me tell you what did happen – that umpire gave Collingwood a free kick last week right in front of the goals, and it cost us the game."

They both moved on with their lives, and the police officer even treated my abuser to another beer due to the absurd accusations made by a woman.

What was the real situation?

Is it ever possible to truly know?

The Native American tale of the two wolves teaches about inner struggle and personal growth. The story revolves around a Cherokee grandfather sharing his wisdom with his grandson. He explains the presence of an ongoing conflict between two wolves within each individual.

Darkness is personified by the original wolf, which includes emotions like greed, arrogance, and guilt. The second wolf symbolises attributes such as light, joy, peace, love, and hope. The grandfather responds to his grandson's question about the winning wolf, saying, "It's the one you decide to feed."

If I don't have a clear understanding of the truth: which narrative should I embrace for the sake of my mental wellbeing?

One whole year had gone by since I first walked into that police station. The objective wasn't his incarceration, but the specific moment of his apprehension. If it wasn't a challenge or any form of humiliating for him, how is that justice?

My belief was that questioning him would make him feel a loss of control and enough fear to ensure the safety of others. I wanted this questioning to hold him accountable for his wrong-doing. I summoned the strength to address the abusive acts he inflicted upon me during my childhood, and I held the belief that the universe would be on my side in seeking justice, even if it was solely in this small way. Did he have a favourable outcome?

I wondered if with a content smile, he reclined in his chair, leisurely sipping his brown beverage, pleased by his success in hiding this secret side from everyone all these years.

This wasn't helping me, these racing thoughts; which direction should I guide them? Now that the worst may be over for him, what aspect should I focus on next? How should I approach this new concept of my happiness is not dependent on his outcome? Do I let my negative thoughts take over, or do I have the bravery to nurture the positive ones filled with light and the potential for happiness in the future for me?

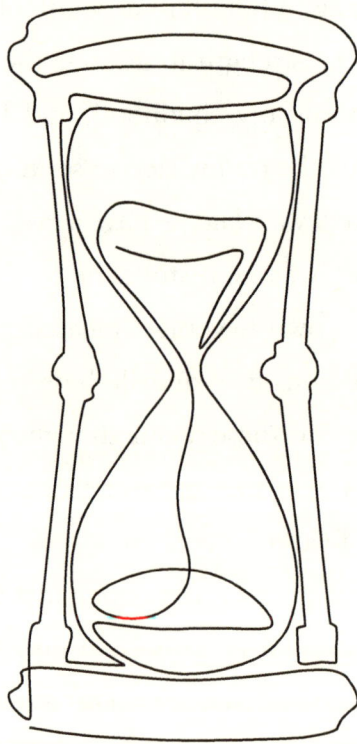

Today I feel lost and sad and confused,

But the police have my story, this truth they will use.

My statement will lead to your inevitable arrest,

My time to stand up and your time to experience unrest.

My time to impart humiliation on you now,

No more questioning by me or understanding the how.

A moment for your strength to be tested this time,

Your vulgarness and actions are yours to define.

Regardless of how far this investigation goes,

It's not our secret anymore, not for just me to know.

Time for the world to see who you really are,

Time for you to know I had the strength to go this far.

Time for you to face all you did to me,

Time for me to step up to all I can be.

I'm handing it over to the universe to take it from here,

I'm standing into my true self as you and the memories
I no longer fear.

Some Days

Some days I would forget this happened to me. Some days, it felt like it was a story I had heard about. Some days I was just Kath; fun, organised, busy Kath who had lots of friends and a happy marriage and a wonderful family – so lucky, so grateful. Other days suddenly it appeared, jumping out like a monster from around a corner to scare me. The day before I had forgotten, and now, I was once again remembering.

While gazing at a childhood photo, compassion engulfed me. I no longer saw a girl defined by her trauma, but one shaped by her strength and resilience. I promised her I would continue to honour her journey – not just with words, but with actions that reflect the healing and empowerment we've achieved together. In reclaiming my power, I found my voice and my purpose. I was lucky.

The puzzle pieces of my life, once disjointed, now formed a cohesive narrative of survival and triumph, illuminating a path forward filled with hope and possibility. The conversation with my abuser, while significant, was but one defining moment in a much larger tapestry of healing and growth. It reinforced the truth that my strength had always been there within me, waiting to be reclaimed. By confronting him, I didn't just speak for the child I once was; I spoke for every part of myself that had endured and persevered through those dark times.

After those four days in bed following that call, I took deliberate steps toward self-care and self-discovery. I immersed myself in mindfulness and meditation to ground my thoughts, attended therapy sessions to continue unpacking my emotions, and engaged in physical activities to reconnect with my body. These practices encompassed more than just recovery; they emphasised embracing a new way of being, from self-love and self-respect.

As the chapters of my life continued to unfold, I found a new rhythm – a delicate balance between acknowledging my past and living fully in the present. Some days it would sneak back, and I would judge myself harshly. But the other days I celebrated my victories, no matter how small, and tried to treat myself with kindness and understanding during setbacks. Conversations with my inner child became a source of immense strength, reminding me of the bravery it took to confront my abuser and the perseverance needed to heal.

This transformation deeply impacted my family as well. We built new traditions based on open communication and mutual support.

My relationships had never been so solid. I know I am lucky, and this isn't everyone's story. I only lost half a family. For many, to face their story means they must walk away from everyone.

How do I ask for something when I don't know what I need?
How can I reach out when I'm locked away and cannot be freed?
I want to open up to you all and ask you to support me.
But the parts that would ask are hidden away and nowhere
to be seen.
I want the pain to disappear, can you help take it away?
I want you to know my truth, but it may be too much for
you to stay.
I sit here in the loneliness and the sorrow of my past.
My life at a standstill while I watch others' success happen fast.
Is life happening to me right now or is it for me in some way?
Time will tell I guess if this pain will dissipate; or is it here
to stay?
If I share with you, can I guarantee that you will stick around,
Not just for all the fun but when my heart is broken on
the ground?
I can't offer much back to you today, which is uncomfortable
to admit.
But all I have will come back to you when I am fighting fit.

Friendship is a journey I'm good at and I give a lot along the way.

But now, I need you to convince me that my loneliness is not here to stay.

So please reach out to me in any way that feels alright for you.

I may not know how to respond, leaning back in is very new.

I have spent a lifetime with a secret that is heavy, dark and cold.

This is a bridge between what I aspire as new and what I know as old.

As I speak out it seems to be creating more separateness in my life.

Not feeling very capable of friendship, motherhood or being a happy wife.

I stand here exposed, alone in my story and I don't want that anymore.

So please come over, say you're here and with gratitude I will open the door.

Chapter Six

The Promise

By this stage, I was tired of being reduced to just a victim, a statistic, a file number. I am a person, with a life, with a story, with value.

Detective four may have praised my resilience, but what about the strength it took to come forward in the first place? What about the courage it takes to relive the trauma over and over again in the hope of finding justice?

All I know about detective four is based on a simple email signature that contained a pronoun: him/he. But you are more than just a gender identity, just as I am more than a survivor of sexual assault. I am defined by my resilience, my strength, my intelligence, my compassion, and so much more. Yet, in the eyes of the law and society, I am often reduced to a mere statistic. It is disheartening to realise that the system is not set up to fully acknowledge the complexity and depth of our experiences as survivors. We are forced to navigate a legal process that often questions our credibility and forces us to prove the validity of our trauma over and over again.

While I strive to be seen as a good human, a dedicated mother, an honest individual, my abuser can simply deny the reality of what transpired. Three simple words: "That didn't happen."

Well, I have two for you: "It did." The injustice of it all is staggering.

While my abuser can simply deny the truth and move on with his life, I am left to carry the weight of his actions for a lifetime. I bear the memories, the trauma, the pain, while he gets to walk away unscathed. It's a heavy burden to bear, one that extends beyond my own wellbeing to impact those closest to me.

I am a resilient witness, possessing intelligence, education, self-awareness, and strength. I stand tall in the face of adversity, armed with the knowledge that I am worth more than the sum of my trauma. I have worked hard, earned my success, and have more financial stability than my abuser. There is no ulterior motive, no hidden agenda in seeking justice – only the pursuit of truth and closure.

In moments of reflection, I can't help but wonder about the different paths my life could have taken. What if I had succumbed to the despair, turned to drugs as a teenager to numb the pain instead of channelling my energy into activities like swimming that brought a healthy purpose? Would I be seen as a credible witness then?

Swimming served as my sanctuary; it enabled me to process emotions that were often beyond my comprehension. Through swimming, I forged a new identity – one defined by strength, speed, and control. It transformed the vulnerable little girl into someone resilient and empowered. In the water, I found a way to drown out the voice that told me I wasn't good enough, using that negativity as motivation to push myself further.

It provided me with a sense of worth and instilled in me the belief that, with hard work, I could achieve anything, even in moments when I felt utterly worthless. The physical exhaustion from swimming ensured that I slept well as a teenager, and my fitness level shielded me from body image concerns.

Looking back, I realise that this sport, along with my decision to pursue it, played a crucial role in saving my life. I will always be thankful to my stepfather for the early morning rides to practice.

Ultimately, I am proud of the choices I have made; more than that, I am eternally grateful I was in a position of privilege to make them.

As the investigation stretched on for 15 long months, every piece of evidence, every testimony gathered was like a thread weaving a complex tapestry of truth. And yet, amidst the vast array of information, there lies a crucial detail that could tip the scales – the admission to an emergency department when I was just 11 years old.

The weight of uncertainty hung heavy in the air as I waited for the final piece of the puzzle, the missing admission record that could change everything. Those words spoken by the detective, promising a chance, a glimmer of hope, were etched in my mind.

For three agonising months, I clung to those words, hoping this journey would lead to the closure and justice I sought. The detective's assurance that things were looking promising, that the evidence was shaping up in our favour, fuelled my determination to see this through to the end.

The detective assured me that he has seen countless cases that have gone to trial with far less evidence than mine, yet the final missing piece could be the linchpin that solidified our stance. With each passing day, each moment of anticipation, the promise seemed to fade away, until finally detective four did too.

In the shadows of injustice, two witnesses stand,
One guided by duty, the other by a trembling hand.
Both have seen the horror, the pain, the despair,
But their paths diverge from that moment of shared air.
The professional witness, with knowledge and skill,
Seeks justice and truth with a steady, firm will.
The drug-addicted witness, lost in a haze,
Haunted by memories, lost in a daze.
Their past, a dark cloud that refuses to fade,
A shattered soul seeking solace in a toxic trade.
One speaks with facts, the other with tears,
One walks in the light, the other in fears.
But beneath the surface, in the depths of their pain,
They both carry wounds that refuse to be slain.
Two witnesses, bound by the chains of abuse,
Navigating a world that's cruel and obtuse.
One seeks redemption, the other seeks peace,
Their stories entwined; their suffering won't cease.
Yet in the tapestry of their shared affliction,
There lies a glimmer of hope, a ray of conviction.
That in their differences, in their paths torn and frayed,
They both hold a courage that can never be swayed.

Three Months' Wait

In those three months waiting for this missing piece of evidence, I found myself oscillating between my need for justice and my need for this all to be over. I was desperately seeking validation for the turmoil this ordeal had put me and my family through. I tried to convince myself that every difficult conversation, every painful memory unearthed, was somehow justified in the grand scheme of things.

I kept telling myself that regardless of the outcome, I would find the strength to endure whatever lay ahead. Just like the moments in life where I had to trust the universe — the nerve-wracking phone call to my abuser, the miracle of giving birth, the seren-dipitous meeting with my husband — I had to trust that this too was a part of some grand design.

I resolved to focus on the belief that if the case did proceed to trial, I had the resilience to weather the storm, and my family had the fortitude to stand by me. Conversely, if there wasn't enough evidence to move forward, I had to trust that we were all being shielded from further harm. It was a struggle to shift my focus from the fear of him escaping consequences, to finding solace in the idea that I was being safeguarded.

I had to remind myself that in the grand scheme of things, justice may not always manifest in the manner we expect, but there was solace in knowing that we were being looked after, one way or another. I had to believe that – if not, what else was there to hold onto?

After the three months was up, I again tried to contact the detective to find out what the outcome was. I called the station and a female officer answered the phone. She sounded rushed and stressed.

What a horrible job these people do every day, I thought. *How do you pick up the phone not knowing what is on the other end of the call, time after time?*

I explained to her that I was chasing up the outcome of my investigation and that I had left several messages and sent several emails but haven't heard anything back. She asked me to hold and was gone for what seemed like an eternity.

When she returned to the call, she sounded different, softer, slower in her speech. What did she know? What was I about to hear?

It was compassion – that is what I heard, that is what I sensed from her. But why?

She informed me that that detective had left the department and was now stationed somewhere else.

She gave me the number and told me to call that station. I did, but was quickly told that the uniformed police officer was out for the moment and would get back to me on his return. What uniformed police officer?

"No, you must have it wrong. I was calling for a detective who works on specialty cases around childhood sexual assault." Once again, I was left waiting.

I stand in this life with composure and flair.

You wouldn't guess beneath the surface I'm lost in a stare.

I am the person you come to when you're feeling down.

I am the person who effortlessly helps shine your crown.

I am the mother who gives all to her children each day.

I am the woman that has slowly given all her spirit away.

I constantly question what the point of all this is.

And if I wasn't here tomorrow, would I really be missed?

Life would go on, maybe a great learning for some.

But my children, oh god, my daughter and son.

I don't know where to go as I am stuck in this bind.

You're standing beside me, and you're completely blind.

My smile is masking the pain that I feel.

My success is all you know to be real.

I keep coming back to this place of fear and loss.
I will keep moving through the days, but at what
personal cost.
My days may be numbered; I am fighting against time.
My crown is on the floor and is in desperate need of a shine.
Will I ever have the strength to tell you how I feel?
Will I ever feel deserving of a life in which I can heal?

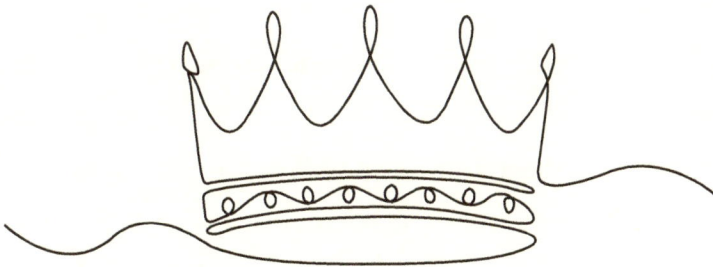

Not an Unusual Story

My story is not an unusual one. I grew up in what would be described as a loving and safe household. Despite this secure and warm environment, my life took a devastating turn when I was just five years old.

I experienced something that shattered my sense of security and changed my life forever. I became one of the millions of children who have been victims of child sexual abuse.

Child sexual abuse is alarmingly prevalent. Approximately one in three girls and one in six boys worldwide experience some form of abuse before the age of 18.[5]

These statistics represent a heartbreaking reality that affects not just the children directly involved, but also their families and communities. Yet, despite its prevalence, child sexual abuse often remains shrouded in secrecy and silence, further compounding the trauma for those who live through it.

From an early age, I found myself in the company of friends who disclosed their own experiences of abuse to me. More friends than I can even begin to recount here shared their stories, speaking of their pain and confusion. These conversations always struck a deep chord within me, resonating with the hidden parts of my own lived experience. It seemed that long before I fully understood my own trauma, I became a confidant to others, a witness to their stories of suffering.

Later in life, I chose a career as a coach, dedicating myself to helping people navigate their challenges and achieve personal growth. As I engaged with my clients, I began to notice a recurring pattern: many of them had their own histories of abuse. They confided in me, shared their deeply personal and painful stories, and sought guidance through their healing journeys.

I often wondered about the nature of this connection. Were they intuitively drawn to me because they sensed I was uniquely equipped to understand and support them? Or was there an unhealed part of me that served as a silent magnet, attracting individuals who had experienced similar trauma? The truth is likely a blend of both.

My personal history of trauma has undoubtedly shaped my empathic abilities and enhanced my capacity to connect deeply with others who have suffered. This shared pain creates a bridge of understanding and trust between us, allowing them to feel seen and heard in ways that perhaps they haven't before.

On the other hand, my own ongoing healing journey might have created an invisible thread that links me to those still seeking solace and resolution for their past wounds. Reflecting on this, I recognise the importance of continuing to heal and grow, not only for my own wellbeing, but also to foster a more supportive and empowering environment for the people I work with.

This self-awareness helps me provide the best possible support to my clients, ensuring that my guidance is grounded in both professional expertise and personal insight, without being clouded by unresolved issues. As I navigate my journey, I strive to transform my experiences into a source of strength and empathy, rather than a point of hidden pain. Engaging in therapy, joining support groups, and participating in continuous self-reflection have all been vital steps in my healing process. These actions not only aid my personal growth, but also enhance my ability to offer genuine and empathetic support to others who have walked similar paths.

The prevalence of child sexual abuse underscores the need for open conversations, widespread education, and robust support systems. By sharing my story and those that have been entrusted to me, I hope to break the silence that often surrounds this issue and encourage a broader dialogue about the impacts of such trauma. It's essential for survivors to know they are not alone and that their experiences, though profoundly painful, do not define their worth or future potential.

For all of us, healing from childhood sexual abuse is a continual process. It involves facing the shadows of our past and integrating those experiences into our lives in a way that diminishes their power over us. Through professional support, personal determination, and community connection, it is possible to rebuild a sense of security and self-worth for all of us.

In the discomfort that divides us, courage takes flight,
To listen, to empathise, to shine a compassionate light.
Addressing sexual violence with an open heart and mind,
Overcoming shame and embarrassment, leaving
judgements behind.

The statistics speak volumes, but behind each number lies a soul,
A person with a story, seeking empathy to make them whole.
One in three girls, one in six boys[6]; their voices need to be heard,
These numbers incomprehensible – completely absurd.

It takes courage to listen, to validate their pain,
To stand in solidarity, their loss to regain.
Support, kindness, and understanding pave the way,
For survivors to heal, to reclaim their sense of sway.

Open dialogues, where truth shines bright,
Teaching our kids to embrace what's right.
Let us be the change, the shift in conversation's tide,
Fostering a culture where courage and compassion abide.

Together, we can bridge the gap, dismantle the divide,
And create a world where survivors no longer hide.
With empathy and understanding, we pave the way,
To a future where all voices matter, each and every day.

Percentages

The vast majority of abuse victims, around 90 per cent, are acquainted with their abuser, particularly in cases of childhood sexual assault. Let me repeat that for you: 90 per cent of sexual assault survivors know their perpetrators. Ninety per cent.

I remember when I first told my mum about the abuse, she said with disbelief, "I thought it was strangers we needed to protect you from." This misconception is one we need to talk about more. This reality creates a profound betrayal as trust is shattered, leading to long-lasting trust issues and complicating healing.

Victims may experience conflicting emotions towards the perpetrator, making it difficult to disclose the abuse and leading to prolonged manipulation and control. So let me share an even more shocking statistic with you: 50 per cent of these sexual abuse cases involve a relative of the victim.[7] A relative, meaning parent, grandparent, uncle, aunt, cousin, or sibling. No wonder only 23 per cent of us ever come forward![8] The fear of familial and social repercussions further discourages reporting, contributing to feelings of isolation and distrust.

I was lucky to have a safe place to share my experiences. Because of my parents' divorce, my brother and I had two separate families that never really collided. My abuser was in one of these families, and my support system in the other family was filled with people that loved, believed, and stood by me.

Would I have come forward if it was a relative on the side of the family I trusted? The honest answer is, I don't know.

The trauma and shame of being abused by someone we know, and that others around you love, is too much to bear. I imagine it's easier to pretend it never happened, to bury it deep inside and try to move on with your life. But the truth is, the effects of childhood sexual abuse can never truly be erased, and it is crucial to seek help and support in order to heal and break the cycle of abuse.

When the abuser is a family member, it creates a deep sense of betrayal. Family is supposed to be a source of safety and trust, a place where you are loved and protected. When that fundamental trust is violated, the emotional fallout can be overwhelming.

This betrayal is felt on multiple levels – personal, emotional, and psychological. It's not just the act itself that is traumatic, but the shattering of the very relationships and foundations that are supposed to hold and support the child.

Because the perpetrator is someone known and loved, there is also a fear of causing disruption or breaking apart the family. Children might fear not being believed or worry about the ramifications of disclosing the abuse. They might think about the pain it could cause other family members, or fear retaliatory actions from the abuser. This fear can reinforce the decision to suppress the memories and stay silent. Pretending it never happened or burying it deep within might seem, on the surface, like a way to move on.

One of the long-term consequences of not addressing these suppressed memories is the risk of perpetuating a cycle of abuse.

Unresolved trauma can impair one's ability to recognise healthy boundaries and maintain stable relationships. It can also lead to maladaptive coping mechanisms such as substance abuse, self-harm, or other risky behaviours.

In some cases, the trauma might even influence parenting styles, potentially affecting the next generation in various harmful ways, potentially at the extremes of overprotective or over-trusting.

I can no longer live in shame; it's time to rise,
I'm shattered and weary, with tear-streaked eyes.
An epidemic of stories, like waves they pour,
An ocean of feelings, tides of fear at the core.

How do we speak of the hurt that we bear?
How do we break the silence that festers despair?
I won't stay hushed just to ease your mind,
I must share my truth; it's my heart's way to unwind.

Please don't twist my tale to reflect your view,
If you can listen and hold space, that is what I need from you.
Can we weather this storm of raw, hurtful pain?
Will our bond withstand the suffocating shame?

Intergenerational Trauma

Intergenerational trauma is a concept that highlights how unresolved trauma from one generation can impact future generations, even if they are never directly abused themselves. Not dealing with your own abuse can have a significant impact on your children, as the trauma you carry may manifest in your behaviours, relationships, and parenting style.

Seeking help and support is essential for several reasons. Firstly, it allows the victim to begin processing and understanding their trauma in a safe environment. Therapists who specialise in trauma can provide strategies for dealing with flashbacks, anxiety, and other symptoms, helping survivors regain control over their lives. This professional support is crucial for breaking the internal cycle of pain and silence that many abuse survivors endure.

Support groups can also be incredibly beneficial. Connecting with others who have had similar experiences can help survivors feel less isolated and more understood. Hearing others' stories can validate their own feelings and experiences, fostering a sense of community and shared strength. These groups often become a safe space to express emotions and work through the trauma collectively.

When I was in Darwin and my abuse had just surfaced, I felt lost. My friends around me did the best they could to support me, and friends and family at home in Melbourne felt helpless being so far away. At the recommendation of my counsellor, I joined a support group.

I wasn't sure if I had the strength to listen to the stories of other people. I was barely holding my own life together, let alone supporting others coping with their own trauma. However, being in a safe space with others who were at different stages of their journey was healing for me. Some were further along, while others like me had just begun. Hearing their stories made me realise that I had only remembered a fraction of what had happened and that I had only allowed myself to face a tiny part of how it had impacted me.

Educating yourself and those close to you about the effects of childhood sexual abuse can be empowering. Knowledge about the psychological and emotional impacts can dispel myths and reduce stigma, making it easier for survivors to seek help without fear of judgement.

Breaking the silence is a powerful step towards healing. Speaking out disrupts the cycle of shame and secrecy that abusers rely on to keep their activities hidden. It also empowers other survivors to come forward, creating a larger network of support and solidarity.

Sharing your story – whether in therapy, a support group, or public advocacy – can be a crucial part of reclaiming your narrative and transforming the pain into a source of strength. Like with my story, when you have been abused by a family member, it is deeply intertwined with feelings of betrayal, shame, and guilt.

This is a man that shares my DNA, what does this say about me? I chose to face this question head on, because I refused to let these acts define me, and more importantly, define the future of my children. Breaking the cycle of abuse starts with breaking the silence. Speaking out about your experiences disrupts the cycle of shame and secrecy, empowering other survivors to come forward and seek help.

It wasn't until I turned 22 and sought help from a psychiatrist that I began to realise the magnitude of what had happened to me. I couldn't remember certain parts of my childhood, and I was struggling to make sense of it all. He told me that "only fruit loops suppress memories", and I didn't strike him as a fruit loop. The psychiatrist's words only added to my confusion and denial.

I would sit with this confusion for 12 months before first the memories of the abuse resurfaced; this was the depression knocking at my door to open them. I was told by several therapists that it was rare to remember my abuse so young when it had been completely suppressed. What is more statistically accurate is individuals who have been abused often are triggered by becoming a parent themselves.

I had a theory about this. You see, I had a test run at parenting. My sister was born when I was 14; she was like a real-life doll to me. I loved her and it was the best age ever to become a big sister.

My brother and I would fight over who got to feed her and pick her outfits. Her whole being would light up when I walked in the room; I don't think I ever felt so loved. This was my first insight into what being a parent might have felt like.

When my memories first surfaced, she was eight – the same age I was when I endured my second incident of abuse. She was sassy, funny, energetic, social, stubborn, and loved people, much like I was at her age. She was just better at asking and getting what she wanted. I always put this down to her being the baby in the family and me being the oldest.

If I took her to get an ice-cream, I would have to say, "Are you sure you want vanilla? I am getting chocolate."

"Yes, I'm sure," until inevitable tears would surface halfway through the ice-cream as she claimed she had changed her mind. This happened so often that I started swaying her to order what I really wanted because I knew swapping ice-creams was how it would pan out.

I felt protective of her like I had never felt about anyone. My brother was only two years younger than me, and we shared a protective nature of one another. I aimed to keep him safe from harm, but he was a boy on a mission for adventure and wouldn't listen to me.

My sister, on the other hand, idolised me, she did listen, or at least I had figured out how to bribe her enough to get her to hear me.

I found myself scanning every teacher, carer, neighbour and family friend to make sure there was no danger lurking around her.

Fortunately for me, she would never have to see anyone on the side of the family where my abuser resided, as she had a different dad to me.

I don't believe that I am unique when my memories surfaced. I just had a sister that mirrored my inner child, just like children do for parents. This opened me up to seeing the abuse from a different perspective, earlier than most.

It opened me up to seeing a clear example of what an eight-year-old child really was: an innocent, harmless, funny, trusting little girl who just wanted love and approval from those she trusted most.

It opened me up to realising that having a memory of ourselves at this age can be morphed and clouded by shame; to love another being that mirrors this age is undeniable in our reality of the imbalance of power and where the shame should reside.

The pain is real, it swallows me whole,
Desperately trying to connect with my soul.
Trying to search for a way to come back,
Finding a way to exit the black.
It is heavy and solid and bigger than me,
The trees from the forest I cannot see.
Other people's needs I can still adhere,
Asking for mine to be filled is something I fear.
My needs are secondary to all in my life,
As a daughter, a friend and even a wife.
"I don't matter" is what screams loud in my mind,
A glimpse, just of flicker of light I wish I could find.
Please show me some evidence that this too will pass,
Please show me some hope so that the pain I can bypass.

Can I do that, can I let it all go?

Can I walk around the pain and connect in with flow?

Or is walking straight through it what I really need?

Is the learning, the growing, the part I should feed?

If the answer is here, then I wish I could see,

If the answer is here, please appear so I can be free.

Free of the dark that's taken over and made me feel numb,

Free me of the dark that's hijacked my potential,

and all I could become.

How can I move from this space I'm in now?

How can love be something I once again can allow?

Right now, today, can I bounce back again?

Or do I just make darkness my friend?

The Outcome

The detective finally called me back. His voice was a jarring blend of regret and resignation. He told me there wasn't enough evidence to move forward with a trial.

"You must have known how hard it would be to get this far," he said, as if to soften the blow. But the words only made my world crumble further. Hard, yes. But impossible, no. How dare he imply it was my fault for not understanding the obstacles.

"I'm sorry," he added. But for what exactly? For neglecting to inform me of this decision for three agonising months? For pretending to be a competent detective when he clearly wasn't? Or perhaps for getting demoted because he failed at his duty? The questions swirled around my mind like a storm, leaving destruction in their wake.

He mentioned the witness who never made a statement, and concluded with, "If only the hospital evidence had turned up, the outcome might have been different." His voice was a drone of "if onlys", a chorus of missed chances and shattered hopes.

"And if only you had of used the word 'rape' 23 years ago when you spoke to your friends, the prosecution says the defence would have had a field day with that discrepancy." Discrepancy? What discrepancy?

"Well," he explained, "the three friends who we interviewed said you remembered that you were abused, but in your witness statement you used the word 'rape'." It had a tone of, *See, it wasn't my fault, it was yours* behind it.

But was he asking me why? I was speechless at the time, but if this is a question here is my answer.

Why was there a discrepancy between my statement and the statement of three separate friends? Because that witness statement was the result of a gruelling four-hour interrogation, where every question peeled away layers of my soul.

Where exactly, what exactly, where exactly again, what exactly again, how exactly – each detail a dagger to my heart, cracking me wide open until there was nothing left but raw truth. A truth that lay buried beneath 23 years of scar tissue.

Yes, *that* witness statement. The one crafted by a 46-year-old woman, armed with wisdom, healing, and unshakable confidence. A woman who had journeyed through hell and emerged with the strength to speak her truth.

Contrast that with the hesitant words of a broken 23-year-old soul, lost in a haze of depression and confusion. A young woman grappling with fragmented memories that invaded her dreams and consumed her days, dragging her further from the light.

Back then, "abused" was all she could muster – the only word my shattered state could manage. It was a dark whisper of fear and sorrow. Abuse at the hands of a relative, a shadow that had begun to choke the life out of me, pulling me away from everything I had known to be true.

I did use the word abused, yes. My friends told the truth, just as I told the truth then and also told the truth 23 years later.

I knew my abuser had hurt me, but it took thousands of hours of therapy to excavate the buried trauma, to understand the full horror of what he had done.

Now, sitting in the suffocating weight of the detective's apology, I realised the true tragedy. Not just the incompetence and lost evidence, but the profound disconnect between my present self and the young woman I used to be. The woman I am now, who can stand tall and own her pain, versus the fragile girl who grappled with the shadowy terror of her past.

So, his apologies ring hollow in my ears, each "if only" and "I'm sorry" a bitter reminder of a failing system. A system that had let down a strong woman seeking justice. A system that failed to be truly trauma-informed.

My truth is my karma, a beacon of light,
Guiding me through darkness, shining bright.
Your lack of justice incidental, I remain tall,
For in the end, my truth will prevail overall.

Speaking up is only the first step,
Being heard is the true healing element.
Knowing that my actions will play their part,
The universe's balance a work of art.

In a poetic justice, sweet and strong,
Letting go of injustice, moving along.
My happiness is my karma, here to stay,
In the rhythm of life, finding my own way.

Relief

As the call with the police officer ended, those empty apologies echoed through the silence, but alongside that ache, there was a glimmer of relief – relief that I had done everything within my power. I had spoken my truth; I had fulfilled my part.

And a profound solace washed over me – relief that I no longer had to summon the strength for a trial. I could finally lay this burden down, and return to my life, to rebuild the parts of me that had been shattered by this revisiting of old wounds.

I could go back to being happy, to finding success, to planning dinner parties and holidays, to dreaming about the next adventure. There would be space for all of it now.

With Covid lockdowns a thing of the past, life was beginning to shift back to normal – a new kind of normal, especially for me. What now? What next? Is that it?

Yes, that chapter was closing. But as it did, the horizon stretched out before me, filled with promise and possibilities. And for the first time in a long while, I felt the stirrings of hope and the quiet, persistent pulse of life calling me forward. I had found my voice, and I was determined to use it.

At 23 I remember.

A new confusion, frozen but frantic.

A dark blanket covers my being.

Then I remember more.

I sit in shame.

Then I become a wife.

I sit in distrust.

Then I become a mother.

I sit in anger.

Then I decide it is not my job to fix this.

I hand it back to you.

I hand it back to all of you

I am So Sorry

Despite the witness to my abuse, another survivor who had also experienced the trauma of assault, not being willing to make a statement, I felt a deep sense of compassion for her. Knowing the pain and suffering she had endured, I understood the difficult position she was in, and my heart ached for her inability to speak out. Our shared experiences of abuse had created a bond between us, a shared understanding of the darkness that can consume a person's soul.

I knew the courage it took to confront the demons of my past, to relive the trauma and speak my truths. And while I respected her decision to remain silent, I couldn't help but feel a sense of sadness that I was never able to help her. I wished I could have been a source of support and strength for her, to offer a listening ear, a shoulder to lean on, and a safe space to share her pain.

I should have said something.

I should have protected you.

But I was a child too.

I am so sorry.

I'm sorry for the silence in which I stood,
While you endured abuse no one ever should.
I should have spoken up, fought for you,
But fear and hesitation held me back, it's true.
I know now the pain and struggle you faced,
And I regret deeply the role I played.
In letting you suffer in silence alone,
I should have been stronger, I should have shown.
I hope you can forgive me for my mistakes,
For the words left unspoken, for the hearts that break.
I carry the burden of regret in my soul,
But I promise to speak up now, to make us both whole.
I'll be your ally, your advocate, your voice,
Standing beside you, making the right choice.
Through this investigation I have been freed,
I will always stand beside you in yours if you need.

Poetic Justice

In the end, the legal system failed to deliver the justice I sought, but the journey itself was a victory. Today, I am choosing to use my voice to advocate for change in the systems that failed me. I know we must work together to establish a safe foundation for understanding, support, and justice for all victims of sexual assault. It is time for change.

The current police process for handling sexual assault cases is outdated and ineffective, often re-traumatising victims in the process. In my experience, the police officers would have benefited from more trauma-informed training.

For example, when I was invited to come into the police station to call my abuser, I shouldn't have been allowed to do this on my own. I know I had to be in the room making the phone call, but I shouldn't have had to drive myself home.

A few months before this call, I had a procedure to fix a frozen shoulder. It was made very clear to me that I wasn't able to have the procedure unless I could ensure that I had someone taking me home, as driving after this was going to be dangerous. The same rule should apply for highly emotional events. Events that require immense courage. Events that can break us wide open.

These individuals that are facilitating these events every day should be educated about how to assist the process to minimise harm to all involved. Officers should be equipped to handle these sensitive situations with empathy and understanding, for their benefit as much as anyone else's.

I understand behaviour, I am trained to understand patterns of thinking. I help individuals to move past unconscious assumptions of one another to better connect in the workplace.

Bias is real for all of us, we can't avoid that our brains make shortcuts and that we are simply a collection of experiences and education that has spanned over our lifetime to get us to see the world a particular way. That is, until we choose to question how we see it. Or until we are educated differently.

I was on a meditation retreat a few years ago and it was a beautiful collection of wise men and women that all had a common goal of growth. We were put into pairs, and I was in a partnership with a man named Peter. He would have been about my dad's age.

I liked him straight away and we had a really in-depth conversation. He praised me for the wisdom I had acquired in my life and in an activity we embarked on together, he saw big things in my future.

It had been such a beautiful day, such a luxury to have some time to myself, and I was so looking forward to an uninterrupted night's sleep. But the sleep never came. It was like something was trying to bust out of me. Something had been unsettled and I couldn't place what it was. It was an anxiety I couldn't shift; I felt like I was in danger, and I couldn't convince my body otherwise.

The next day, I was emotional and frustrated. I was having an internal conversation – *wasn't that why I was here*, I told myself, *for growth?* I knew growth wasn't a comfortable process. People all around me were having breakthroughs and learnings about themselves and I just felt BLAHH… Tired and now emotional and grumpy.

I should have just gone to a day spa and sipped on wine while I read a book, that would have been a break! Despite the lingering thoughts that I had made a mistake by coming to this retreat, I persevered. Later that day, I was faced with a reality I wasn't expecting.

I was concerned that the upcoming presentation I had scheduled was out of my depth. I was to present on the topic of unconscious bias to a room full of white, middle-aged men. The irony wasn't lost on me, and therefore I was concerned that the content wouldn't land.

The facilitator started an activity that involved calling out a person's name and then asking them to play a role.

Ben – Now jump up and in front of the group pretend to be a French waiter.

Sarah – You jump up now and pretend to be a principal at a private English school.

Kath – Now you jump up in front of the group and pretend to play a powerful presenter speaking on the topic of unconscious bias.

Oh, he was good. What a clever way for me to push through my fears. I took a deep breath and said "*Okay*, but first I need to leave the room and come back in as her." I was emotional, tired and confused about what had been unsettled inside of me.

I got out of my chair, and I walked out the door. I looked up at the sky and I breathed, connecting with the strength, energy and presence that I knew I could conjure when required. I came back into the room with the confidence of my professional self.

I asked the facilitator if he could move to make room for me to have the stage; he smiled and stepped aside. And then I did a three-minute presentation about unconscious bias; it flowed out of me with confidence and power. Later I was told that I was unrecognisable to the group in that moment – I had transformed into something or someone else.

When I was done, I took a breath and stepped back into my presence as a participant. They applauded and showered me with praise. Some of that praise came from Peter, the man that I had been partnered with the previous day.

When I looked up, he looked in that moment like my abuser, but had the gentleness of my mum's brother who was one of the most beautiful men I had ever met. *How can he remind me of both these men at the same time?* I burst into tears.

Then I shared with him that I was having trouble reconciling that he could look like my abuser and be such a nice person. And there it was: my bias for the room to see, for me to see. This is what I had been unhinged by the day before. I had to face my own bias about men before I could possibly have an impact presenting this content.

Did I know my stuff? Yes. Was I good at holding the attention of a room? Yes. Did I believe I was in danger with men older than me? Yes, most of the time, until they proved otherwise. That was my breakthrough – one of many that keep coming.

My justice is poetic, a tale of my youth,
My weapon of choice, speaking and writing truth.
My voice was once silenced, in a period of strife,
But through hard work, I've unlocked its life.

I speak for the voiceless, the marginalised that seek,
Using words as my weapon, to fight powers bleak.
Through poetry and phrase, my message is clear,
Justice and healing is what we hold dear.

So, let's raise our voices, in unison and song,
For the silenced and oppressed, we must stand strong.
With hard work and healing, we'll pave the way,
For a world where justice and truth will forever stay.

Bias

It made me think, *What were the assumptions that were accumulated over time by police officers that were faced with the worst of humanity every day?*

What were the assumptions made about me by simply hearing my story? What was the bias that underpinned their decision making? *Her life isn't so bad, the abuse must not have been either?*

We are all multifaceted and more than one event, more than one moment of time; one piece of learning can't define us. To ensure this is not shaping how we experience the world around us, we must accept that we have to keep questioning our thoughts; we have to create space between thoughts and action. To master this, we have to do the work on ourselves, so that we avoid being triggered by unresolved trauma and accumulated experiences.

Victims of sexual assault endure a harrowing journey, not just through the traumatic experience itself, but also through the daunting process of seeking justice. Throughout this intricate and emotionally taxing investigation process, it is essential that survivors receive comprehensive support and guidance every step of the way.

I understood that my response to the phone call to my abuser was dissociating from my body; I asked for a councillor, and I told her how to help me. "Put me back into myself," I asked. I knew that I needed to have my nervous system realigned before I went home to my family, back into a Covid lockdown with nowhere to go.

So, I broke the rules and went to a woman's house for healing. But most people in that situation don't know what they need. The police should tell them what they need, or they should have someone advising them to help them discover it themselves. The unfortunate reality is that resources for victims are often scarce and inaccessible.

I encountered a staggering six-month waiting list for a counsellor, compelling me to take matters into my own hands and finance my therapy myself because I didn't want to take a position from someone who didn't have that option. This disparity highlights a critical flaw in our system – every survivor deserves swift and unrestricted access to the critical support services they require to heal and rebuild their lives.

Friends of mine have spent their lives travelling the world. I spent my money and spare time learning, healing, growing, traveling to the various aspects of my trauma to heal. I shouldn't be punished for that choice any more than someone who didn't have the resources to do the same.

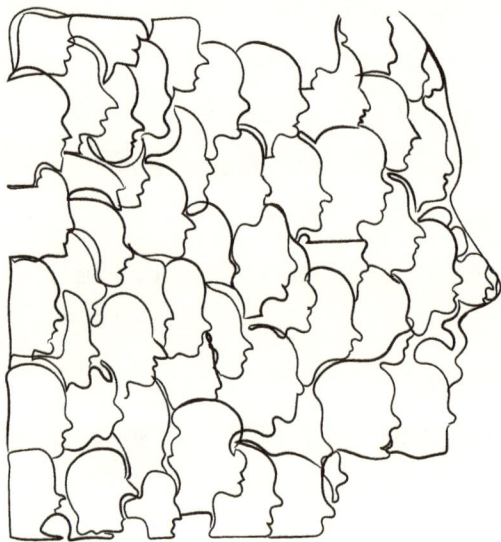

Bias and judgement, they tear us apart,
Creating divisions in every heart.
I succeed because of my past pain,
She sells her body, her scars not in vain.

You wear the badge, but your past haunts your mind,
We're all just trying to survive, trying to find,
A way to move forward, to heal and to grow,
But bias and judgement, they make it hard to flow.

Chapter Seven

Shame

Despite finding peace with my own story, I am constantly reminded of the shortcomings and injustices that many survivors of sexual assault face in their journey towards healing and justice. Reflecting on my experience, I often wonder about the many "what ifs" that could have made a difference in my own path to healing and recovery.

Overcoming shame and embarrassment is a crucial step in addressing the uncomfortable but necessary conversation surrounding sexual violence and abuse. Shame is often misplaced and carried by victims. Shame creates discomfort that often enables a barrier, preventing us from openly discussing and confronting the harsh realities that so many individuals face.

It is only by acknowledging and addressing this discomfort that we can begin to bridge the gap and create a more supportive and empathetic society. So how do we do that? We must put our discomfort aside and have the courage to listen.

When the statistics of one in three girls and one in six boys who experience sexual abuse[9] represent real people with real stories – they are not just numbers but husbands, wives, mothers, fathers, siblings, and friends who need our unwavering support and compassion.

It takes courage to listen to their experiences, to validate their feelings, and to stand alongside them in their journey towards healing and justice. Support, listening, courage, and kindness are the cornerstones of building a community that is responsive and empathetic to survivors of sexual violence.

By offering our presence, our understanding, and our empathy, we can create a safe space for survivors to share their stories, seek help, and begin the process of healing. It is through these acts of kindness and compassion that lives can be saved, and transformation can occur.

It begins small. It is time to change the conversation we are having with our children and loved ones. Instead of sweeping uncomfortable topics under the rug or trying to shield them from harsh realities, let us be open, honest, and vulnerable in our discussions.

Let us show our children that it is okay to be seen and to see others in a vulnerable state — that true connection and understanding come from embracing all parts of ourselves and each other. By breaking the silence, we can create a world where survivors are supported, where perpetrators are held accountable, and where all individuals can feel heard.

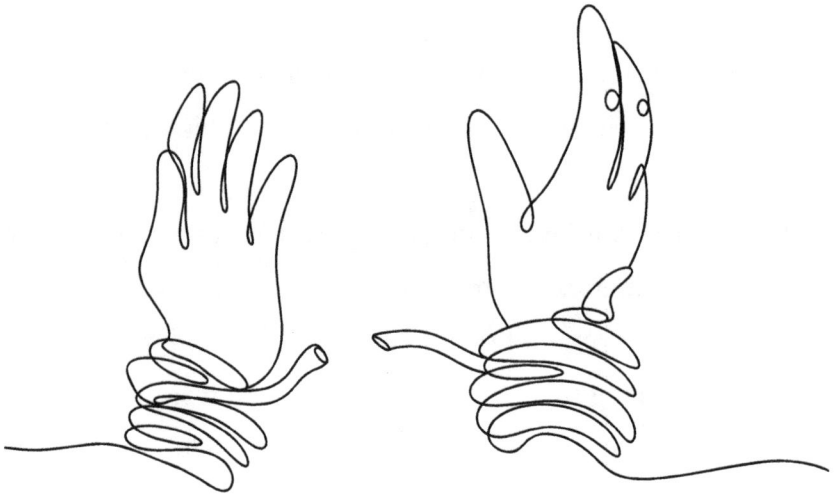

In the shadows where silence lies,
Whispers of pain and stifled cries.
A darkness lingers, unseen and cold,
Where secrets hide and stories unfold.

But we rise, a force strong and true,
To change the narrative, to renew.
No more blame or shame to bear,
Together we'll break the chains of despair.

Let's shift the conversation, start anew,
Empathy and understanding, let them shine through.
For survivors of abuse, a light in the night,
Their voices heard; their spirits take flight.

It's time to align, hand in hand,
And create a world where we understand.
Where love and respect are the guiding flame,
And together, we'll end the cycle of shame.

Trigger Warning

In our quest for meaningful connections, it is essential to cultivate a sense of responsibility and safeguard our own wellbeing in order to nurture genuine relationships with others.

Amid the challenges brought by the pandemic, I was running a corporate workshop with a group of professionals during a virtual gathering. During this discussion, I used a photo of Grace Tame as an example of how we make snap judgements and assumptions with seven seconds.

She was the celebrated Australian of the Year at that time and was extensively portrayed in the media, but the photo I used was when she was younger, and I contrasted this against one where she was empowered and celebrated. No reference to why she was Australian of the Year was mentioned in this example.

Following the session, a participant reached out via email to share her personal reflections:

"Dear Kath, I joined your presentation today using my personal email. Your delivery was exceptional, and the content deeply resonated with me; however, it stirred up distress within me. As someone who has survived prolonged sexual abuse, seeing a photo of Grace Tame without warning triggered emotional pain from my traumatic past. This is not a critique of your professionalism or knowledge but stems from my own experiences. The overall presentation left a lasting impact and offered valuable insights. Thank you."

In response to her message, I expressed gratitude for her openness and courage in sharing her story:

"I am thankful for your honesty and willingness to share your perspective with me. It saddens me to hear about the hardships you have faced. Drawing from my own journey as a survivor of sexual assault, I use Grace Tame as an example not to cause harm but to recognise the strength and resilience she possesses." I continued on about how our life experiences mould us. I shared with her how I had to personally overcome my biases against men and how it poses an ongoing internal battle for me.

In her response, she expressed gratitude also:

"Thank you for your prompt reply, Kath. Reflecting on our interaction, I realise that my reaction was influenced more by personal sensitivity than any shortcomings in your presentation style. Given my past encounters with trauma-related issues while teaching Community Services students, I approach trigger warnings with great care. Upon reflection, I now realise that the precautions taken may have seemed excessive, given the extensive coverage of this topic in mainstream media. Your courage in openly sharing your story with an audience predominantly composed of men from diverse professional backgrounds is truly admirable and inspiring."

I trust we both learnt from this interaction; I certainly did. How much do I share and how much do I hide for the comfort of others? This sparked my curiosity about the concept of trigger warnings and how I could approach my training sessions to acknowledge that everyone has a story without causing distress for the audience, especially since I was conducting training for professionals in a workplace setting.

In the intricate tapestry of human connections, stimuli constantly awaken deep-seated emotions and memories. So how do we connect without triggering each other? Is it even possible? Growth is uncomfortable after all.

A wise mentor once imparted a profound wisdom: these triggers are omnipresent, affecting individuals in various ways – from a woman reeling from the aftermath of a divorce stumbling upon anniversary celebrations in a Facebook post, to someone grappling with illness being confronted by images of vibrant health.

I myself was deeply impacted by discussions of pregnancies and newborn babies while suffering multiple miscarriages. But while I was triggered, was it the responsibility of others around me to shield me from these conversations? I was also hurt when I was excluded from them, so it was lose-lose for those around me trying to do the right thing.

Experiencing triggers involves encountering intense emotional or psychological responses, often negative, triggered by specific stimuli or situations reminiscent of past traumas or distressing events. This can result in feelings of distress, anger, anxiety, or sadness and may even manifest physically through symptoms like increased heart rate, sweating, or difficulty breathing.

Manoeuvring through a world rife with triggers necessitates striking a balance between understanding others' narratives and challenges, while holding ourselves accountable for our responses. There have been various studies on the effectiveness of trigger warnings.

In one such study, the findings were "that trigger warnings had no meaningful effect on response affect, avoidance, or educational outcomes (i.e., comprehension). However, trigger warnings reliably increased anticipatory distress before viewing material."[10]

It also stated that "Contrary to both views, we found that warnings had no effect on emotional reactions to material. That is, existing published research almost unanimously suggests that trigger warnings do not mitigate distress."[11]

Trigger warnings have been proven to create avoidance and avoidance can be considered the opposite to healing. It is within this crossroads that authentic comprehension and personal development blossom. Progress towards tranquillity and recovery involves engaging in tough dialogues within us and with others. It calls for a willingness to listen, learn, and evolve, fostering a culture founded on mutual esteem and comprehension.

Oprah Winfrey's impactful work, "What Happened to You?", underscores the significance of lending an empathetic ear to those who have endured trauma without passing judgement. When existing systems fail to provide victims with a platform to voice their experiences, it becomes our duty to construct environments where their voices are honoured and validated.

As algorithms feed us agreeable information constantly, embracing attentive listening is key to promoting shared healing and growth. Recognising our role in interactions is crucial for personal growth and gaining deeper understanding. Valuing diverse viewpoints and engaging in mindful communication helps us navigate life's complexities. Avoiding perspectives and attitudes we disagree with or that trigger us limits our ability to grow and learn.

I wrote a letter to my future self at the tender age of 12, a poignant reminder of the challenges faced in childhood and the profound impact of friendship on our existence. In this letter, I begged my future self to never forget how hard it is to be 12, to not be invited to a party, to not be selected for the front row of the dance concert. To not get to play centre for a game of netball and be put in defence instead.

It was these things that made me cry myself to sleep, that allowed the tears to wet my pillow, not the abuse; as a parent, I try to remember that. The innocence of youth often magnifies seemingly minor events, emphasising the significance of compassion and awareness towards each other's life experiences. My learning through this is that very often the issue at hand is not the one that is driving the emotion.

Traumas from our past can resurface unexpectedly, engulfing us in waves of emotions that transport us back to those difficult moments. Whether it be a panic attack during a school gathering or sleepless nights after witnessing distressing scenes on TV, these triggers hold significant sway over our emotional wellbeing.

I am terrified of the exposure my children and this generation have online. I know that the issues they will face as a result will not be known for years to come, that is a different conversation but an equally important one to have.

What I am referring to here is adults who are aware of their trauma being asked to stay silent because it is too uncomfortable for other adults to hear what they have to say. While avoidance may offer temporary reprieve, it ultimately feeds into anxiety and fear about confronting our deepest fears.

When the brain's emotional centre is activated, it doesn't just recall a past event but re-lives it as if it were happening in the present moment. I have experienced this firsthand, triggered by instances that led me back to my childhood abuse without conscious awareness.

Reflecting on a time during grade six when I had a panic attack during a sex education session at school, I remember feeling overwhelmed with an intense urge to escape. Without understanding what was triggering me, I abruptly left the room midway through the session, citing nausea as an excuse. Reflecting on this moment, and others like it, prompts me to question: would a trigger warning have made a difference when my mind was not consciously aware of the source of my distress?

Could the teacher have seen this as an opportunity to reach out or speak to my parents about my reaction, considering I was the only one from memory who did react this way?

Part of my healing when my memories first surfaced was reading everything I could find about abuse. Was this a form of desensitising, was it making sense of something that seems so implausible? Avoidance never works; walking gently can. Find your pace; be okay that those around you are also just doing their best at navigating their own internal struggles. If something is triggering you, it's a knock to remind you that it is taking energy; it is a nudge that it's ready to be let go of.

Don't settle for carrying this around the rest of your life. Pain is pain, the weight it has can be lightened. We must choose to be responsible for our responses to the world around us. This doesn't mean self-blame for our reactions or projected blame for others, it means to just notice what is triggering emotion with compassion. This is not for those around us to manage but for us to notice.

I acknowledge that we all have unique journeys to healing, mine has been one where I have faced the topic head on to aspire to make sense of it all. I am assuming if you are still reading at this point in the book, education and truth are important to you too. Go gently, walk your way and I trust together that the conversation can expand to give survivors a voice.

I am 12 sitting amidst my peers,
Talk of anatomy drawing cheers,
But my body begins to tremble,
As laughter and jokes assemble.

My mind is a chaotic mess,
Organs wanting to confess,
Breath becoming shallow and quick,
Panic rising, feeling sick.

"Help," I silently plea,
Feeling like I can't breathe,
Why do I feel like I'm dying,
What's wrong with me, I'm crying.

I must be a frigid, I must be a prude,
Boys laughing, teacher thinks I'm rude,
The talk of anatomy too much to bear,
Feeling like I'm lost, not even there.

Mind, Body, Soul

What if the professional I confided in had referred me to a counsellor instead of dismissively labelling me as a "fruit loop"? The impact of such a simple gesture could have been profound, providing me with the support and guidance I desperately needed at that moment. Instead, of circling the drain into a dark hole of depression. The impact of a simple yet crucial gesture, such as being referred to a counsellor when confiding in a professional, cannot be overstated.

It could have been a turning point in my journey towards healing and justice. Instead of feeling dismissed and marginalised by being labelled a derogatory term like "fruit loop," being connected with a counsellor could have provided me with the support and guidance that was essential for me to understand earlier the trauma I had experienced.

I was lucky to have found support along the way through various modalities. If you are navigating this healing yourself, understand the journey will take trial and error every step of the way. My journey of healing feels like an onion being peeling back piece by piece. One layer of healing sometimes highlights a new layer of trauma. One life experience or stage brings with it new learnings and challenges.

I found that what worked for me in one layer of healing didn't work for the next, so I always had a foot in both Eastern and

Western camps. Aside from family and friends, these are the things that helped me along the way, all at differing times, in all varieties of ways.

Mind

The mind, where thoughts and emotions reside,
Holding memories, where healing must abide.
Processing trauma, fostering resilience,
Creating space for newfound brilliance.

- Psychologist
- Psychiatrist
- Counsellor
- Rape crisis centre
- Relationships Australia
- Life coaching
- Conversions
- Support groups
- Helplines
- Watching movies
- Documentaries about trauma
- Movies about overcoming adversity
- Reading books
- Psychotherapy
- Listening to podcasts
- Medication
- NLP
- Family constellation therapy
- Journaling
- Book clubs where you drink wine

Body

The body, a vessel that carries our pain,
The physical manifestation of the mind's gain.
Releasing tension, finding release,
Through movement and care, a sense of peace.

- Swimming
- Walking
- Running
- Cooking
- Eating
- Yoga
- Hiking
- Gardening
- Forest bathing
- Dancing
- Cleaning my house
- Shopping for clothes that made me feel empowered
- Being strong and fit
- Herbal medicine
- Naturopathy
- Acupuncture
- Traditional Chinese medicine
- Massage
- Reflexology
- Pilates
- Spa
- Sauna
- Cold water therapy (but I am better in the warm)

Spirit

The spirit, our inner essence and light,
Connecting to purpose, shining bright.
Nurturing faith, hope, and love,
An anchor in turmoil, a force from above.

- Reiki
- Qi gong
- Equine therapy
- Art healing
- Card readings
- Past life work
- Inner child work
- Screaming in my car
- Singing in my car
- Women's circle
- Chakra balancing
- Shamanic healing
- Breathwork
- Sound healing
- Kinesiology
- Craniosacral therapy
- Live music
- Energy healing
- Listening to Enya
- Aromatherapy
- Mindfulness
- Drawing
- Poetry
- The ocean
- The sand on bare feet
- Watching the clouds in the sky
- Dancing
- Girls' weekends

In the moment of vulnerability, I sought solace and respite,
Confiding in a professional, hoping for guidance and light.
But instead of support, I was met with a dismissive label,
A hurtful term that left me feeling unstable.

What if, in that crucial moment, a different path was taken,
And a counsellor was recommended, my spirit not forsaken?
The impact of such a simple gesture, profound and deep,
Could have been the lifeline I needed, the promise I seek
A counsellor's expertise, a sanctuary for my pain,
A safe space to unpack, to heal and regain.

The power of connection, of empathy and care,
Could have lifted me up, shown me that someone is there.
To listen, to guide, to walk by my side,
To help me navigate the storm, to reclaim my pride.

So let us remember the impact of a single kind deed,
And strive to be the support that others may need.
To offer solace and hope, a helping hand and an ear,
To create a world where healing and justice are near.

The Language We Use

What if our legal system acknowledged the significant healing required for survivors to shift from the word "abuse" to "rape" and used this understanding to validate our stories rather than discredit them? The power of validation and acknowledgment cannot be underestimated in the journey towards justice and healing.

My personal journey from the word "abuse" to acknowledging and using the term "rape" was significant. These represent more than words; they represent how comfortable I was with my own story and how uncomfortable I understood it would make others.

I see the word "abuse" like the choose-your-own-adventure books I would read as a kid. People around me could insert their own version of what that meant to them, depending on their own comfort. They could direct their own experience by turning the page that they choose, not one I would direct them to.

Unfortunately, what this meant was that my obscurity created distance between myself and others. I was expecting a level of support from people based on very little information I was sharing. It wasn't actually until speaking about this publicly that many people close to me learnt of the depth of my story. I am sorry I didn't trust earlier that you could hear it. Maybe the walls that were present between us may not have needed to exist at all.

Language represents a crucial step in validating our experiences and reclaiming our power. The lack of acknowledgment and understanding within our legal system regarding this transition in language was detrimental to my pursuit of justice.

When the legal system can acknowledge the immense healing required to shift from using the word "abuse" to recognising and naming the experience as "rape", it will signal a monumental shift in how society views and responds to sexual violence. By understanding the complexities and nuances of trauma and the transformative process survivors undergo in reclaiming their narratives, the legal system could play a pivotal role in validating survivors' stories and affirming their right to seek justice.

The power of validation and acknowledgment in the legal system cannot be underestimated. It has the potential to shift the narrative around sexual violence, challenge victim-blaming attitudes, and foster a culture of support and belief for survivors.

In the courtroom, in the halls of justice and law,
The impact of validation, a crucial flaw.
Survivors' stories deserve to be heard and believed,
To shift the conversation, to change how we perceive.
By acknowledging the journey survivors undertake,
From 'abuse' to 'rape', from silence to awake,
The legal system can be a force for good and support,
Validating their experiences, justice as the ultimate port.
Let us strive for a system that validates and uplifts,
The voices of survivors, their truths, their shifts.

Predator

We need to collectively change the narrative around what a predator looks like and where the danger for our children statistically resides. By challenging stereotypes and misconceptions, we can better protect and educate our communities about the realities of sexual violence and abuse.

One of the first steps in this process is to move away from the traditional image of a predator as a stranger lurking in the shadows. While this scenario can and does happen, the majority of sexual assaults are actually committed by someone known to the victim – a family member, a friend, a teacher, a coach, or another individual who holds a position of trust and authority, or in childhood, it can also be a peer. By acknowledging this reality, we can better equip ourselves to recognise the signs of potential abuse and take proactive measures to prevent harm.

Education is key in changing the narrative around sexual violence and abuse. By providing age-appropriate information and resources to children and adults alike, we can empower individuals to recognise and respond to potentially dangerous situations, while also fostering a greater sense of empathy, respect, and consent within our communities.

These "what ifs" serve as a reminder of the work that still needs to be done to create a more supportive and understanding environment for survivors of sexual assault.

I may have found peace within my story, but the wound is still there. Focusing on the fact that it can serve as a catalyst for change and advocacy for others who are still searching for their own sense of healing and justice is what gives me this peace.

What if we dared to change the tale we tell,
Of predators lurking, unseen, where they dwell?
What if we shattered the myths and the lies,
To safeguard our children, to open our eyes?

Challenging stereotypes, misconceptions untold,
To educate, protect, in our arms to enfold.
By unveiling the truth, we break through the haze,
To illuminate the shadows, to guide our ways.

No longer just strangers, but those we hold dear,
The danger may lurk where it's least clear.
From family and friends, to figures of trust,
We must learn to discern, to confront, to adjust.

No blame on the victim, no shame to endure,
It's time to shift focus, to seek a cure.
The fault lies not with the wounded and scarred,
But with those who inflict pain, who we often disregard.

Education, empowerment, knowledge to share,
To instil in our communities, a culture fair.
With understanding, compassion, and consent as our creed,
We build a world where all are safe and freed.

Cognitive Dissonance

Cognitive dissonance, as a psychological term, refers to the mental discomfort or tension that arises from holding contradictory beliefs, attitudes, or behaviours. This discrepancy between what a person believes, and their actions or other beliefs, can lead to feelings of discomfort, leading them to try and resolve or rationalise the inconsistency. People may experience cognitive dissonance when they encounter information that challenges their existing beliefs or when they behave in ways that contradict their values.

The term was coined by psychologist Leon Festinger in the 1950s. Cognitive dissonance can play a significant role in how individuals, including survivors, perpetrators, and society, respond to childhood sexual assault cases.

For survivors of childhood sexual assault, cognitive dissonance may manifest as conflicting emotions and beliefs about what happened to them. They may struggle with feelings of shame, self-blame, and guilt, as well as fear of repercussions or disbelief from others. These internal conflicts can cause psychological distress and hinder the survivor's ability to come forward and seek help.

Perpetrators of childhood sexual assault may also experience cognitive dissonance in various ways. They may rationalise their actions, minimise the harm caused, or deny accountability to reduce the mental discomfort of acknowledging their wrongdoing.

In society, cognitive dissonance may be evident in how childhood sexual assault cases are perceived and addressed. There may be a tendency to blame and stigmatise survivors, dismiss their experiences, or downplay the seriousness of the abuse to maintain existing beliefs or societal norms. This cognitive dissonance can perpetuate harmful attitudes and barriers to justice for survivors.

By recognising and addressing cognitive dissonance, stakeholders can work towards creating a more supportive, empathetic, and accountable response to survivors of childhood sexual assault.

When a relative is the perpetrator of childhood sexual abuse, cognitive dissonance can manifest in particularly complex and challenging ways for both the survivor and the family members involved.

For the survivor, who may have had a close and trusting relationship with the relative, cognitive dissonance can arise from the conflicting emotions of love and fear, trust and betrayal, and the struggle to reconcile the abuse with their previous positive feelings towards the abuser. This internal conflict can lead to feelings of confusion, self-blame, and a sense of shattered trust and safety. Survivors may also face pressure from other family members to keep the abuse a secret or to protect the abuser, further contributing to their internal turmoil.

Family members who become aware of the abuse or have suspicions of abuse may also grapple with this. They may experience conflicting beliefs about their relative's behaviour, the survivor's disclosures, and their own role in addressing the abuse. They may struggle with feelings of loyalty, denial, or the desire to protect the family unit, leading to challenges in supporting the survivor and holding the perpetrator accountable.

A great example of this is a show I recently watched on ABC called 'After the Party'.

'After the Party' is a poignant exploration of family dynamics, trust, and the complexities of relationships. The show delves into the life of a beloved family man, whose seemingly perfect image is disrupted by serious accusations made by his wife.

This narrative often prompts an examination of societal perceptions of blame, especially in cases involving gender dynamics and the expectations placed on women to bear the burden of family secrets.

Throughout the series, viewers are invited to empathise with both partners. The husband's character embodies the facade of a perfect life, while the wife emerges as a figure struggling with her emotions, caught between loyalty and her own reality. This dual perspective encourages audiences to consider the profound impact of public perception versus private truth.

As the plot unfolds, the show raises important questions: What does it mean to truly know someone? How do societal norms shape our understanding of blame and victimhood?

Through its character development and narrative arcs, 'After the Party' challenges viewers to scrutinise their own assumptions and biases about relationships and accountability. Ultimately, it's a powerful reminder of how easily perception can be manipulated by what we think we know and the importance of listening to all voices in a story.

In the realm of minds, where beliefs collide,

Cognitive dissonance resides inside.

A tension brews from contradictions deep,

Cracks in the foundation where beliefs seep.

Shame, blame, and fear all intertwine,

As cognitive dissonance clouds the mind.

Society, a mirror reflecting back,

Casts a shadow on the truths we lack.

Victims blamed, their voices dimmed,

As dissonance weaves a tapestry grim.

Cognitive dissonance, a spectre profound,

In the hurt that echoes, in silence bound.

He Was Once a Boy

In my studies over the years, I have experienced an exercise that opened my eyes to the complexity of healing and all its multi-layered facets. It was a guided meditation where my five-year-old self-met my abuser's five-year-old self.

It had a profound effect on me. After only ever encountering him as an adult, I forgot that he was once a child. This exercise aims to evoke empathy and compassion by considering the potential experiences and influences that may have shaped your perpetrator's actions. I had a need to understand and make sense of this, which has been part of my healing.

I know that this is not for everyone, but it helped me let go of some anger which of course is the aim of healing after all. The healing process was never forgiveness for his peace, but acceptance for mine.

A small boy once, innocent and pure,

Loved his parents, climbed trees for sure.

Where did you falter, where did you stray,

From that child's path, led astray?

What shadows darkened your tender heart,

What demons lurked, what tore you apart?

Why did you keep silent, hide the truth,

The pain you carried from your youth.

If only you had shared the tales untold,

The secrets kept the pain you hold.

Now I stand, healed and whole,

No longer victim to your cruel control.

I've found my voice, my strength, my light,

In the darkness, I emerged, I took flight.

No thanks to you, I found my way,

To a brighter, happier, pain-free day.

May you too find the courage to break free,

From the chains that bind, from your own agony.

Inner Child

Through the sharing of my personal journey, I have come to realise that true healing does not stem solely from vocalising our struggles, but from deeply connecting with and giving a voice to all aspects of ourselves.

Throughout my healing, many pivotal moments have found me unprepared.

One such moment was when my daughter turned five. Leading up to this birthday, it was easy to justify that the tiredness was from my year with another newborn baby in the house, as my son was turning one at the same time.

As a working mother, it is easy to justify stress and feeling overwhelmed with life, so I wasn't looking for the obvious reason why I was not sleeping or struggling to keep my anxiety at bay.

While I was writing a birthday card for my daughter, sharing with her how proud I was of the brave, funny and independent little girl she was, the tears started streaming down my face. Planning her fifth birthday party was an emotional and harrowing experience, until I invited my own five-year-old self to come along for the journey. I invited my five-year-old self to express all her anger, frustration and hurt for her birthday being tarnished by the acts of an adult who she should have been able to trust.

I invited her to let go of all the hurt by sharing with me her sadness, my adult self who now had the capacity not only to listen to her, but to tell her all the things that she needed to hear.

It wasn't your fault. I'm so sorry that happened to you. You were just a child. It was your birthday. You should have been able to just play on the swing, eat cake and unwrap your presents. That is what a five-year-old should do at their party. So come along to this one, let's plan it together. You can share this experience, and I will keep you safe.

So, she came along to the party for my daughter and stood beside me through every moment of girly goodness. She smiled as the children brought in their dolls to put into the tent with spare nappies and toys.

My five-year-old self loved playing dolls. She smiled as the kids all painted bibs for their babies. My five-year-old self loved painting. She brimmed with joy as the children ate cake. My five-year-old self was given a second chance at feeling safe to do so.

It could have gone in a very different direction. This inner child, if not heard, could have sabotaged the whole thing for my daughter and for me. But instead, I listened to her pain and filled it with a new experience that healed both the mother within and the inner child standing alongside.

It is imperative for us to pause and consider whose voices we may be neglecting to hear in our lives – be it those of loved ones, acquaintances, or even our own inner voice. Without tuning inwards to our own truths and vulnerabilities, we hinder our capacity to truly connect with others.

Grant forgiveness to the child within, extend grace to the adults who may have overlooked your cries, not for their benefit, but for your own liberation and peace. You are deserving of acknowledging and embracing every facet of your being.

This wasn't the only time my inner child stopped me in my tracks. When my daughter turned eight, the same creeping sensation of aloneness came over me like a dark cloud.

A pivotal step in our journey towards healing involves acknowledging and nurturing our inner child, who houses our most profound emotions and wounds.

My five-year-old self-had been heard, it was now time for my eight-year-old self to have the same acknowledgement. Her needs were different.

The emotions this eight-year-old self was housing were different.

Confusion: *How has he got away with this, with my whole family there again?*

Fear: *Will this happen again?*

Belief: *I am never safe.*

Anger: *It's up to me to keep myself safe; no adults know what is happening.*

By tuning into this inner sanctuary, we can address and heal the traumas that hinder our personal growth and wellbeing. One part of the onion being peeled allowed for a new level to surface. This inner child required different healing, a different conversation and more work. I asked her what she needed to feel safe. I gave her space to feel angry. I needed space to retreat as her natural inclination was to distract herself by looking after others. She needed to look after herself this time.

I took her shopping, we did our nails, we wrote poetry, we coloured in, we played with our fairy cards. We joined a women's circle and learnt about tarot cards. I used a Ouija board and spoke to my grandmothers, who both told me to write. So here I am, writing – and it began with my eight-year-old self, screaming to be heard. So, I listened. Every day I listen.

It is essential to prioritise hearing and embracing our own needs and desires, fostering self-compassion, and deepening our self-understanding. By honing in on our innermost thoughts and feelings, we nurture a profound connection with ourselves and lay the groundwork for self-love and acceptance. Through the act of sharing our narratives and experiences, we not only inspire others to engage in active listening, but also spark a ripple effect of empowerment and healing for others.

I know the healing I have done has freed my daughter from carrying the same beliefs that have been established as a result of this abuse. That is the fundamental motivation for going to the police.

My 11-year-old self was the one that needed that. That is where the rape occurred. This was a crime; this was an unimaginable crime that needed to be given space to be punished. That is what she needed: fairness, justice. The need for communicating right and wrong. The need to share that there was someone else that had been hurt also. I had to speak up for her too.

The emotions knocking:

Shame – *deep, unimaginable shame.*

Guilt – *I should have known better, why did I ever go to stay there?*

The overarching sense that this was all my fault clouded this 11-year-old self's mind. I don't know that I would have survived watching my daughter turn that age without doing the work first.

So, a wisdom, a higher wisdom carried me into the police station that day and allowed her to be heard, all of my younger selves to be heard. Beyond the witness statement, beyond the phone call, but the check-ins by family and friends, taking them on the journey with me, with all the parts of me.

When we courageously commit to truly hearing and acknowledging one another, we collectively create a fortified, nurturing environment for ourselves and future generations. My children witnessed vulnerability and strength.

My inner child is now embracing the freedom of sharing the load and experiencing the joy when your own story can gently and respectfully be brought along for the ride. As we collectively embrace the valour to listen to ourselves and be heard by others, we fortify our bonds. This is how we pave the way for a brighter tomorrow for the generations yet to come.

In the depths of our soul, a child resides,
With innocence and wonder, they confide.
In dreams and memories, they still play,
But their pain and sorrow never stray.

They carry wounds from days of old,
Scars and hurts that never quite fold.
Their voice is silenced, but still cries,
For love and acceptance in disguise.

To heal and grow, we must go back,
To listen and acknowledge what they lack.
Their fears and joys, we must embrace,
To let them know they have a place.

In doing so, we set them free,
From the chains of their history.
Their light shines bright, once again,
And we find healing in the end.

So, honour your inner child's voice,
For in it lies your truest choice.
To heal and love, to grow and soar,
And unlock the light forevermore.

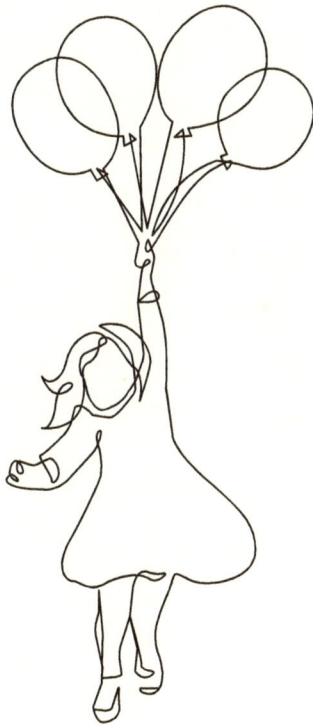

Writing

What has become clear to me over the past few years is that the ultimate goal here is not speaking up, but feeling heard. This means all parts of you must feel heard for you to experience the peace we all deserve.

Writing has been a significant source of healing for me, allowing me to reclaim my narrative and find solace in my journey towards wholeness. Through various writing exercises, I focused on connecting with my inner child and addressing the impact of childhood sexual assault. Through this work, I have discovered a profound sense of empowerment and self-compassion.

These activities have provided a safe space for me to express my emotions, reflect on past experiences, and nurture a deeper understanding of myself. By engaging in these exercises, I have found a transformative way to process my trauma, embrace resilience, and foster a renewed sense of strength and healing.

In the quiet space of listening,
Where words can fade away,
We find a sense of validation,
In what our hearts convey.

Feeling heard is a gentle gift,
That whispers to our soul,
It tells us that we matter,
And helps us feel whole.

When our experiences are acknowledged,
And our feelings are embraced,
We find a connection that binds us,
In a warm, comforting embrace.

By tuning in to our inner child,
And listening to our guide within,
We uncover a source of wisdom,
That speaks of where we've been.

When others lend a listening ear,
And truly hear our voice,
We feel a sense of empowerment,
And the courage to make our choice.

Feeling heard is a precious treasure,
That enriches our sense of self,
It builds a staircase to confidence,
And puts doubts on a shelf.

So let us listen to our hearts,
And honour our truth inside,
For when we feel heard and understood,
Our spirits can truly glide.

Impact Statement

One of the most powerful pieces of writing an individual can produce is a victim impact statement that is read out to the accused in court.

Because statistically most of our cases will never proceed from an investigation into a trial, it also means we won't get a chance to read this statement to the person or people who hurt us. However, that doesn't mean we can't still write one. That doesn't mean that we can't express our experience. Even if you were to write and burn it for no one else to ever read, the process of finding your voice for you is important.

To conclude this book, I would like to share with you my impact statement.

Maybe my abuser will read this, maybe his wife will or his children or another person he hurt, or maybe they never will. That isn't the point of it. The important part to me is that you are reading it. And that I have written it, expressed my feelings and let them go.

I want to thank you for reading this book and hearing my story. I trust you have done this for one of two reasons: you are a survivor of sexual abuse yourself, or you are supporting someone who is.

I am writing this book because I would have loved something to read to validate my feelings as they were arising throughout my journey. If you are a survivor yourself, I trust this book has done this for you. I want you to know how brave you are still navigating the stormy sea of trauma, however your story has unfolded.

Please share your experience so you are not so alone in this. There is support when you are ready. If speaking to your family or friends is too much, go to a professional for assistance. But please speak to someone; this is too much to carry alone, and you deserve to feel heard.

If you are along the path of your journey like me and have already done years of therapy and are interested in going to the police, these are the things I would love you to know that I didn't.

1. You can go to the police and give an initial statement without ever pressing charges. I didn't know that. I might have done it sooner if I did.

2. You can start an investigation and put it on hold until you are ready to go back to it at any time.

3. The investigation happens where the incidents occurred, not where you now live, start at your local police station.

4. Even though the likelihood of going to trial is slim, I benefited from the process of handing it over and letting it go.

5. It is not a step for everyone, so you need to be clear on your own objectives. Mine was about confronting my abuser, so I used the investigation to do this.

6. I still believe that some information in the system is better than nothing. How that we possibly empower police to make a difference if they don't have all the information?

7. You can start an investigation and never go back to it.

8. You and your needs are all that matter; do it for you if you need it, not because others need justice for you.

9. Have a team of support around you and allow them to be your mirror to help you if you are going off track. I would recommend writing to them to ask permission to seek support before you need it.

10. Justice looks different for everyone. For me it was about speaking up and standing strong, for you it might be privately processing and using a trained therapist to work through it. Know what you need and give that to yourself.

I would have loved an opportunity to share a book like this with my family and friends, who often struggled to understand what I was going through.

If you are a support person, thank you so much for what you are doing and for reading this. Look after yourself in the process; get your own support. None of us are unscathed when we see someone we love in pain.

This is a complex subject. This is an emotional topic to navigate, particularly when involving a perpetrator you know. Do the work yourself to process the feelings that arise for you during this time.

Let all the anger, guilt and shame pour out so you can be an empty vessel. Allow the storm of emotions within you to pour out like rain, so that you can become a clear, calm lake for the person you are helping to find solace and support.

I don't like the idea of calling this piece of writing a victim impact statement. It's okay if it resonates with you, but for me, it is a survivor impact statement that feels more aligned with where I would like this message to land. So here I go...

Dear abuser,

Standing at the crossroads of my existence, I trace the Map of my journey, marked by the scars you left behind. Each wound shapes my perception of the world, and I have emerged, ready to share my truth.

Shame once chained me in isolation, echoing the unworthiness you projected onto me. But that shame was never mine; it is yours alone to bear. In my darkest days, it wasn't death itself I craved; rather, I longed for an escape from the suffering that overshadowed my existence. Now, I dismantle that illusion of inadequacy and reclaim the flame of courage that refuses to be extinguished.

I have shed the Mask of doubt you imposed and refuse to hide any longer. These acts of a grown man who wielded power over a small child are despicable. No longer cowering in silence, I reclaim my voice, emerging as a vibrant mosaic of my being.

I will not allow your violence to define me. While I do not excuse the pain you inflicted, I honour the resilience I have conjured from these experiences. Through the eyes of those who love me, I see a tapestry woven from my struggles and triumphs, a reminder of my intrinsic worth.

It is heartbreaking that those we trust exploit family bonds. Shame on you for betraying us all. As I open my heart to love, I wonder — do you know its warmth? I stand tall and proud of my choices, while your actions highlight inadequacies.

I refuse to be a victim; I choose to model resilience and strength for my children, showing them that trauma can heal and be left in the past. I stride through my history unburned while you remain engulfed in your intergenerational inadequacy.

I invite you to confront my reflection – a reminder of the strength you sought to extinguish. These actions must be brought out of the shadows and into the light to foster change for future generations. If my story is a catalyst for the voices of many, then I am no longer a piece of your puzzle; you are now just a small part of mine.

With strength from all the parts of me that need to be heard,

Survivor

Thank you for reading until the end.
As a gesture of gratitude, I want to provide you with
a tool to assist you in expressing your own experience.

On my website, you'll find a free resource to
help you craft your Survivor Impact Statement.

Reflect on your journey and use this tool
to share your experiences.

Your voice matters, and sharing your story is a
decisive step towards healing and empowerment.

www.bespeak.au/book-bonus

Acknowledgements

I sincerely thank everyone who has been a part of my journey and supported me.

To the amazing women in my life, I feel incredibly fortunate to have a family filled with strength and generosity: my aunties, grandmothers, and cousins, who feel like sisters to me. Your unwavering support has given me the safe and loving family many only dream of. My childhood was graced with kindness and love, overcoming any difficult moments I faced; not everyone is as lucky as I am.

To Libby and Brydie, thank you for creating a space for us in a place where we didn't belong.

To my Mum, from whom I have gained my strength, grit, organisational skills, compassion, and passion for helping others in need, thank you for your endless support.

To my sister, who has been my apprenticeship in parenting and is now my closest friend, I love you dearly.

To my friend, spiritual mentor and guide, Cathy. Words cannot and will not be enough to say thank you or express my appreciation for you and who you have been in my life.

To my closest friends from school – you know your significant impact on my life. You stood by me during painful times, reminding me of who I am beyond the trauma. You held up the mirror that helped me see I could keep going, and I am forever grateful for that.

Having such wonderful lifelong friends means I don't need to seek more, yet new friendships continue to flourish. My life at the beach is filled with friends with whom I have shared laughter, tears, and dances. You mean everything to me and have become the family I rely on daily. It's hard not to name you all; you know who you are.

Now, let's talk about the men in my life.

Wayno, you and your meditation group have played a key role in my healing and finding my voice. Thank you to everyone who has held space for me through the years; I have gained so much from you all.

To my dad, I forgive you. I'm sorry you never had the chance to confront your pain, whatever it was. I recognise you did your best with what you knew. Thank you for giving me a wonderful sense of humour and a generous spirit. May you rest in peace; the pain ends with me.

To my stepdad, Pete, thank you for giving me a safe home and supporting my mum during our struggles. Your presence has had a significant impact on our lives.

To my brother, what a rocky journey we've walked together. You are one of the kindest people I know. Thank you for standing by me as I left my abuser's family, for moving to Darwin to support me, and for all the meals you've cooked to cheer me up. I wish you nothing but love and happiness (and maybe another Essendon Premiership!)

Now, onto my children.

To my daughter, you are my teacher. My inner child thrives alongside you during birthday parties, shopping trips, and dance-offs. I consider myself lucky to have you, and I'm constantly learning to be better, stronger, and more courageous from you. Keep being you; you are incredible and will bring greatness. Your authenticity has healed parts of me; I couldn't have done it any other way.

To my son, you are like a recipe of kindness, humour, commitment, competitiveness, and compassion. You will undoubtedly win over many hearts; be kind to them all. Your determination inspires me. Continue chasing your dreams, and let your heart guide you.

Pride seems inadequate to express how I feel about being a mother to both of you.

This is my poem of thanks: Stay Salty…

May you always soak in the sun's gentle embrace,
Even when it's hidden, its warmth finds a place.
As clouds drift by, softening your view,
Remember, behind them, your brilliance shines through.
Stay salty, my dear – like the sea's wild dance,
Let the waves wash over you, take a chance.
With each ebb and flow, let go of the weight,
Dive deep into waters where hope opens the gate.
Be kind to yourselves; be tender, be true,
For nestled within is a strength that shines through.
You come from good stock, so spread goodness around,
You owe the world nothing, but joy will abound.
Your soul will awaken with each kind deed done,
As you stroll down this path where love's light won.
So extend that goodness; let joy be your song,
In this journey together, where we all truly belong.

To my husband's parents, thank you for bringing such a kind, hardworking, and loyal man into the world. He is so lucky to have you as his parents; the kids and I are blessed to have you, too.

To my husband, you see me fully; you experience both the worst and the best of me. Thank you for always supporting my grand ideas with unwavering belief. You have faith in my strength, and I know this story may be hard for you to hear. Thank you for being strong enough to stand alongside me, as I tell it. Your support has been invaluable, and our love has helped me find the courage to share my truth. For that, I know that I am extremely lucky.

www.bespeak.au   instagram.com/kath_essing

About the Author

Kath, a courageous author, speaker, and educator. With a passion for empowering others to embrace their authentic selves, she transforms difficult conversations into powerful moments of connection. Drawing from her extensive background in coaching, mindfulness, and psychotherapy, Kath promotes opportunities to shift the narrative to enable a greater sense of belonging to oneself and beyond.

In her debut book, *Journey to Self*, Kath guided thousands on their paths to confront internal struggles, prompting her own journey to break free from her own silence. A silence she had maintained for years in her misguided comfort of others. This profound self-reflection birthed this latest memoir, where she bravely shares her story of remembering, recovering, and reporting her childhood sexual abuse as an adult survivor. Through her heartfelt narrative, Kath seeks to inspire others and reshape the discourse surrounding this critical issue, alleviating feelings of isolation and encouraging healing. With her innovative framework, "Shifting the Narrative," and engaging workshops, Kath empowers individuals to overcome their inner challenges and reclaim their voices, sparking meaningful change within themselves and their broader communities. Her unwavering commitment to healing and connection continues to leave a positive impact on everyone she encounters, lighting the way for a brighter, more empathetic world.

Endnotes

1 Unicef, 'Sexual violence against children', June 2022, https://www.unicef.org/protection/sexual-violence-against-children

2 BlueKnot Foundation 'Facts and Figures' (n.d), https://blueknot.org.au/resources/facts-and-figures/

3 Finkelhor, D. & Ormrod, R. (2000). Characteristics of Crimes Against Juveniles. Juvenile Justice Bulletin. (Publication No. NCJ 179034). Washington, DC: U.S. Department of Justice, Office of Justice Programs, Office of Juvenile Justice and Delinquency Prevention.
Australian Bureau of Statistics (2022), 'Crime and Justice – Sexual Violence' https://www.abs.gov.au/statistics/people/crime-and-justice/sexual-violence/latest-release

4 Singh, A., Morrison, B. W., & Morrison, N. M. V. (2023). Psychologist attitudes towards disclosure and believability of childhood sexual abuse: Can biases affect perception, judgement, and action?. *Child abuse & neglect, 146*, 106506. https://doi.org/10.1016/j.chiabu.2023.106506

5 BlueKnot Foundation 'Facts and Figures' (n.d), https://blueknot.org.au/resources/facts-and-figures/

6 ibid.

7 Australian Institute for Health and Welfare, 'Family, domestic and sexual violence', 19 July 2024, [online]https://www.aihw.gov.au/family-domestic-and-sexual-violence/types-of-violence/child-sexual-abuse

8 Australian Institute for Health and Welfare, 'Family, domestic and sexual violence', 19 July 2024, [online]https://www.aihw.gov.au/family-domestic-and-sexual-violence/types-of-violence/child-sexual-abuse

9 BlueKnot Foundation 'Facts and Figures' (n.d), https://blueknot.org.au/resources/facts-and-figures/

10 Bridgland, Victoria & Jones, Payton & Bellet, Benjamin. (2022). A Meta-Analysis of the Effects of Trigger Warnings, Content Warnings, and Content Notes. 10.31219/osf.io/qav9m.

11 ibid.

Audiobook

The Courage to Speak Your Truth is also available in audio format.

Jump onto your favourite audiobook platform to have the story narrated for you by the woman who wrote it.

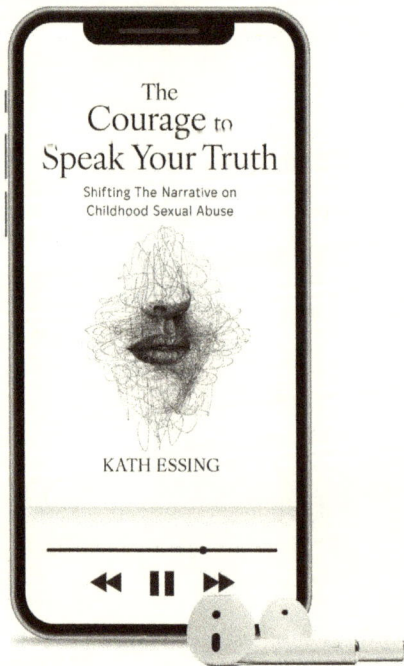

audible
an amazon company

Spotify

The
Courage to
Speak Your Truth

Shifting The Narrative on
Childhood Sexual Abuse

KATH ESSING

www.ingramcontent.com/pod-product-compliance
Lightning Source LLC
Chambersburg PA
CBHW031940090426
42811CB00002B/250